Narnia

Narnia
Unlocking the Wardrobe

Paul A. Karkainen

SPIRE

Published by Fleming H. Revell
a division of Baker Publishing Group
P.O. Box 6287, Grand Rapids, MI 49516-6287
www.revellbooks.com

Spire edition published 2007
ISBN 10: 0-8007-8760-9
ISBN 978-0-8007-8760-8

Previously published under the title *Narnia Explored*

Printed in the United States of America

To my dad, who showed me, through his crippled body, the meaning of courage and perseverance, and for whom the holidays truly have begun.

Contents

Introduction

More than fifty years ago, a professor of English literature named C. S. Lewis created the fantasy world of Narnia. Since then, generations of readers have found the Chronicles of Narnia unending sources of inspiration and delight.

For many authors, the fantasy novel may seem childish and unworthy of attention, but Lewis understood the human need for such imaginative tales, and he brought to them the combination of the depth of one of the finest minds of England and the heart of a child. The unique result was the Chronicles of Narnia. This seven-book series tells the story of the imaginary land of Narnia and the children who discover it. Each story is enjoyable and perfectly understandable for children, yet there is a deeper level of meaning that is best understood by adults. And now a major motion picture has translated the magic of Narnia into a vivid, visual portrayal of four memorable children and the great lion, Aslan, who permeates their world and changes it forever.

Narnia has multiple meanings for the millions of people who have been touched by the books, and now also for those who have been inspired by the film adaptation of *The Lion, the Witch and the Wardrobe*. Fantasy lovers revel in the world of talking animals and mythological creatures. Those who are concerned about moral drift focus more on the character-building events and lessons that appear in every story. Yet it is the looming presence of Aslan that dominates these books. Narnia without Aslan would be a world without a soul.

From the time Aslan is first introduced by Mr. Beaver in *The Lion, the Witch and the Wardrobe*, every character is either drawn to or repelled by the very mention of his name. For some, a strange feeling "like the first signs of spring, like good news, had come over them." It is Aslan who transforms Narnia from a merely entertaining world to a place where the audience must either accept or reject the divine presence of the king of beasts in a world of talking animals.

Narnia is, in fact, a spiritual country—a place that is rich with meaning and filled with the rumor of God's presence. In our world, it is all too easy to wander aimlessly from day to day without acknowledging God's importance in our lives. We place great value on earning a living, making friends, accumulating things, and avoiding trouble, but all too seldom do we wonder about the eternal purpose for which God created us. In Narnia, the children must choose between following Aslan or the White Witch, just as we must decide whether to serve God or listen to the clamorous voices of secular society. When the children choose to follow Aslan, the very air of Narnia works to make them braver, stronger, and wiser. We too can inhale the oxygen-rich air from God's Spirit.

At first, the children believe that only in Narnia can they experience friendship with the lordly lion. However, at the end of *The Voyage of the* Dawn Treader, Aslan makes it clear that he can be found in our world as well. "It isn't Narnia, you know," sobs Lucy. "It's *you*. We shan't meet *you* there. And how can we live never meeting *you*?" Aslan replies that Lucy will meet him in our world. "But there I have another name. You must learn to know me by that name." He further explains that she was brought into Narnia so that, by knowing Aslan a little there, she could know him better here. Christians will recognize that Aslan's name in our world is Jesus Christ.

Aslan clearly represents what Jesus would be like in a world of talking animals. For example, one overarching theme is that Aslan is not a tame lion. As Mr. Beaver explains it, Aslan is not safe, but he is good. He is fierce with the Witch; kind and gentle with Lucy (who loves him the most); terrifying with the talking horse, Bree, who needs the motivation of Aslan's roars and claws to keep him moving; and always understanding what every character needs at the moment.

There are telling truths and wonderfully portrayed lessons in every book. In *The Lion, the Witch and the Wardrobe*, the deep magic established by the Emperor-

Over-Sea requires a willing (and worthy) victim to give up his life to pay for another's treachery, and deeper magic makes death itself work backward and become life again. *Prince Caspian* emphasizes the necessity of following Aslan instead of conventional wisdom in order to achieve one's destiny. In *The Voyage of the Dawn Treader*, the power of Aslan strips the dragonish character out of a very egotistical, cowardly, and boorish boy. *The Silver Chair* shows the vital importance of obeying Aslan's signs in order to penetrate the poison-green witch's underground realm and free the enchanted prince. *The Horse and His Boy* illustrates the importance of humility and the folly of making false assumptions about someone's character based on appearances. *The Magician's Nephew* describes the terrible price of following one's thirst for knowledge at all costs. Finally, *The Last Battle* demonstrates that truth can be distorted and evil is powerful, but all worlds will eventually come to the end that God has decreed for them. Therefore, all soulish creatures (people and talking beasts) must "take the adventure that Aslan sends."

The purpose of *Narnia: Unlocking the Wardrobe* is to show how Aslan's presence permeates the world of Narnia, and how following Jesus in our world lifts us from being horizontal creatures who never look up to being happy, fulfilled inhabitants of Christ's divine kingdom. I aim to ferret out the wisdom on every page of the Chronicles and show how these timeless tales reflect the Christian worldview of C. S. Lewis.

Narnia should be read one chapter at a time. Watch the movies as they are released, or read one of the seven Narnia books, before reading the corresponding chapter in this book. The Chronicles of Narnia richly repay endless rereadings with new insights. Every page is filled with eternal truth and a fresh perspective into the abundant life that God offers to all who seek Him with their whole hearts. Like Lucy, we must fall in love with the God who has come down to live among us and embrace the joy and fulfillment that He offers to all who accept Him as Lord and Savior.

1

The Magician's Nephew

The call of the occult is strong in this world. From the daily horoscope read by millions of people to the First Church of Satan, people are dabbling in, laughing at, entertaining themselves with, being subtly influenced by, and becoming deeply enmeshed in the lure of magic. To many, it is a game. Their thinking runs this way: *Why not find out what the stars hold in store for today? If they tell me something good, it will improve my disposition and my attitude toward my wife and my secretary. If the message is negative, I can laugh it off. Besides, it doesn't hurt me to be a little cautious every so often. Who knows? There could be a scientific explanation for some of the amazing stories people tell about their horoscopes.*

When astrology becomes a little tame, there are other forms of occult diversion. Surely a black Sabbath is more interesting than a boring Sunday sermon. And there are no hang-ups with rules. A man can be a warlock and a sinner, too. And look at that cute witch down the block! If she's mixed up in magic, it can't be that bad.

That's the way a surprisingly large number of people argue. Hal Lindsey has observed the same phenomenon, and he claims in his book *There's a New World Coming* that the great whore, Babylon, portrayed in Revelation 17 and 18, is really the world movement of the occult. He traces the history of astrology back to the ancient Babylonians who, he says, built the tower of Babel so that they could see the heavens more clearly. Whatever its origin, an interest in magic and astrology has existed through the ages. In the last few years, however, it has achieved heights of popularity not known since the Renaissance. Lewis's book *The Magician's Nephew*, though it predates the current fad, describes the movement and its adherents with a precision born of personal experience. Lewis, in his younger days, felt the tug toward forbidden things and knew the deadly attraction as well as the selfish blindness of that siren call.

The Call of the Occult

Lewis chose a very ordinary magician, Digory's Uncle Andrew, to show what the occult is really like. For every Jadis, who is strikingly beautiful and courageous, as well as selfish and exploitative, there are a thousand Andrews, who only go as far as they think they safely can but flatter themselves on being fearless creatures. Uncle Andrew is a gaunt, aging man who lives off his sister and has impoverished her in the process. He does not even talk to her, except to ask for a loan or relief from his many debts. He is a parasite, but he considers it his due.

Uncle Andrew is interested in Digory as a guinea pig for an experiment he wants to conduct. When Digory and Polly suddenly appear in his study, Uncle Andrew first considers forcing them to help him. Then he concocts a vicious little scheme to compel Digory's participation: he tricks Polly into touching a yellow ring, which makes her disappear.

Most of the key characteristics of the magic-minded person are revealed in that initial encounter. Uncle Andrew makes it clear that he is above the rules. He believes that moral standards apply to other people, but not to himself. Rules are for "little boys—and servants—and women—and even people in general," but they do not apply to "profound students and great thinkers and sages." He claims that his devotion to magic separates him both from common rules and from common pleasures. Then he quotes the motto of the magician: "Ours, my boy, is a high and lonely destiny."

As in most of Satan's utterances, there is a mixture of truth and falsehood in Uncle Andrew's words. People who dabble in magic really do cut themselves off from simple pleasures, but not for the reason they think. The fact is that magic ruins one's ability to enjoy love or ice cream or baseball or a sunset. Nothing pleases except more of the forbidden art, and that pleasure is transitory. Edmund discovered in *The Lion, the Witch and the Wardrobe* that nothing spoils the appetite for good ordinary food like bad magic food. But people who play around with magic pretend that their failure to respond to ordinary activities is a result of their devotion to something they claim benefits others as well as themselves. They act as if they are sacrificing themselves for the human race.

Actually, they are making a virtue of necessity. Like the drug addict, more and more of the forbidden substance is needed to produce the same illicit thrill. They are slaves to anything Satan might suggest as a means of producing that thrill. They are willing to suffer pain and deprivation to escape from the ennui that comes after their artificially induced high wears off. Uncle Andrew's fairy godmother is instructive in this regard. He tells us that Mrs. Lefay (which means "the fairy") became progressively less able to bear ordinary people in her later life. She did more and more things that Uncle Andrew considered "unwise," until finally she was thrown into jail. It is interesting that he is quick to point out that she was not confined to a mental asylum, which, for some reason, has much more of a stigma for him than jail does. Apparently, he believes that magicians are mentally competent, regardless of the liberties they must take with the law. But Mrs. Lefay's experimentation could not bring her happiness, and neither can Uncle Andrew's. And even Digory can see through his uncle's justification for moral deviation. Digory's summation of the situation applies to all magicians: "All it means . . . is that he thinks he can do anything he likes to get anything he wants."

Whether one is cautious or not, a devotion to the occult always exacts a price. Uncle Andrew has to make the acquaintance of "some devilish queer people, and go through some very disagreeable experiences" that turn his hair gray, in order to discover the secret of his Atlantean box. Fear forms a large part of the world of magic—fear of what must be suffered to learn horrible secrets, fear of one's fellow practitioners (who are not such very nice people), and fear of the authorities when society's rules are bent and broken. People talk a great deal of the guilt and fear imposed on Christians, but those who go beyond the pale for their pleasures face a much more oppressive load of terror and rejection. There is no fear greater than that experienced by the person who has cut himself off from society's protection by disobeying society's rules.

Lewis even makes a plug for antivivisection in *The Magician's Nephew*. Uncle Andrew uses live guinea pigs for experiments with the dust from his Atlantean box. Lewis did not approve of the use of live animals for cruel experiments, even in the interest of science. It is difficult not to be sympathetic with his viewpoint, when you think about guinea pigs exploding "like little bombs." Uncle Andrew's practice of vivisection has made him hate and fear animals, so that he is unable to appreciate Narnian talking animals as anything other than ferocious wild beasts that need to be shot by a courageous big-game hunter (which obviously eliminates Uncle Andrew).

Uncle Andrew says that he learned by examining it that the Atlantean box "wasn't Greek, or Old Egyptian, or Babylonian, or Hittite, or Chinese." This emphasizes the point made in Hal Lindsey's book that certain cultures throughout the ages have emphasized and passed along the black arts. Lindsey specifically mentions several nations referred to by Uncle Andrew. The point is that the lure of the forbidden and unknown has intrigued men throughout history. Today's upsurge in occult practices parallels those of previous centuries.

The key characteristic of the magician is selfishness. Uncle Andrew is typical in this respect. He looks for subjects to do his experiments on, but he doesn't even consider involving himself. He is shocked when Digory suggests he should be sending himself to the other world via a yellow ring, rather than looking for human guinea pigs like Digory and Polly to send. Uncle Andrew claims that his old age, poor health, and the dangers of the journey make this a ridiculous suggestion. But he totally fails to appreciate the danger to others. The fact is that he doesn't care. He is the magician conducting the experiment, and he requires subjects to practice on. He babbles on about sacrifice, but the sacrifice involves others, if at all possible, and not himself. He is the general sending others off to fight his wars. Digory sees through this ruse and only agrees to go along with the experiment because he realizes he must in order to save Polly. Although they themselves are not virtuous, magicians are good at exploiting the virtues of others. As a parting shot, however, Digory displays the courage Uncle Andrew lacks by telling him he is a wicked magician and will get his just deserts in the end. The fact that Uncle Andrew is willing to use the weakened condition of Digory's mother as a lever to force Digory to do things shows the truth of Digory's assessment.

One other fact about magic becomes clear after Digory and Polly leave this world: Magicians don't really understand the things they fool with. Uncle Andrew knows nothing about the Wood between the Worlds, which is the other world to which he sends Digory and Polly. Moreover, he doesn't even understand the true nature of the rings he gives them. He thinks the yellow rings are outward rings and the green rings are homeward rings. Actually, the yellow rings draw wearers into the Wood between the Worlds, and green rings send them into another world when they jump into its pool.

Uncle Andrew is not the only one who feels the call of the occult in this book. His nephew, Digory, also has the sort of mentality that is attracted by strange knowledge. Digory nearly dooms Polly and himself to a lifetime of wandering, by rushing away to explore other worlds before marking the pool which leads to earth. Polly reminds him just in time, but his hand shakes with fright as he realizes how foolish he has been.

When the two children reach the world of Charn, the call of the occult once more overcomes Digory. As he enters Charn's hall of ancestors, he can feel the strong influence of magic, but he doesn't guard against its influence. He reads Jadis's taunting invitation to strike the little golden bell with the little golden hammer and is immediately sucked in. Magic gives him the ability to read the poem written in a strange language, and magic gives him the wild curiosity to learn what will happen if he strikes the bell. The witch's poem symbolizes the call of the occult. It dares the reader to strike the bell, acknowledges the danger in doing so, but claims that curiosity will drive him mad if he resists.

Practitioners of witchcraft use the same appeal to draw people into the maelstrom of magic. They never deny that their calling is difficult and dangerous, but they claim that only they really know about the areas of life that are really important—those beyond the mundane concerns of ordinary people. One of the purposes of this book is to show that their interpretation is wrong.

When Digory decides to take the fatal step, he lets nothing stand in his way. When he puts down Polly because she is a girl, she says that he looks exactly like his uncle. He even goes beyond his uncle's tactics by using force to keep her from leaving Charn. A really nasty tone comes into his voice when he speaks to Polly; he hurts her wrist when he grabs her; and, in ringing the bell, he brings the curse of Jadis on them, on London, and on the world of Narnia. Digory is not confirmed in evil, even as he does these things, but that does not stop him from being used by Satan.

The bell produces a sweet but horrible sound that wakes Jadis and ruins the palace at Charn. That sound may be heard today. There are subtle voices all around telling man he can perfect his world and bring in an era of peace and prosperity. Some of these voices are sincere, but others are masking a vaulting ambition with sweet lies. So many people have an angle they want to play. They play the game of flattering those around them so they can gain the support needed to establish their place in the world. Their voices may be sweet, but there is something horrible about what they say.

Uncle Andrew is the typical amateur magician dabbling in the occult without understanding it, and Digory is typical of the believer interrupted and betrayed in the middle of a worthy endeavor by a too-active curiosity. But the witch Jadis of Charn, as Digory observes, is the real thing: a magician whose magic is in her blood, not in rules and books. One service that she unwittingly performs for Digory is to show him how paltry his uncle's attempts at magic really are. Once Jadis appears on the scene, Uncle Andrew becomes comic relief—a cowardly, mindless buffoon who flatters himself that the witch will fall in love with him when she is away, but grovels in abject horror when she is present.

Jadis is the last scion of a noble family, which took a decided turn for the worse long before Jadis was born. The history of her house is fascinating in itself. The earliest representatives in the hall of ancestors seem kind and wise; they were obviously good rulers. Their successors are simply stern; they probably lived by the rules and expected their subjects to do the same, but there was no joy in that activity. Doing their duty was the sum of their lives, but they knew no joy. These kings and queens are uncomfortably reminiscent of certain stages in church history, when law swallowed up grace.

The legalistic kings and queens in Charn's history were succeeded by rulers who were strong and proud and happy but also cruel. These people probably stopped obeying the rules themselves, and that is what made them happy. But they were probably still imposing the rules on others, and that made them cruel and selfish. They represent the first fruition of hypocrisy. Legalism led to hypocrisy in Charn, just as it does in this world. Those who extend the Lord's commands far beyond what He ever intended eventually produce offspring who pay lip service to the system but cheat whenever possible.

Once selfishness comes to the fore, cruelty becomes more and more prominent. People no longer believe in a moral code or in the God who stands behind the code. So they oppress their fellow man every chance they get. Charn's rulers lost the joy they derived from abandoning the moral code. Nothing mattered except being on top, and they did worse and worse things to attain that position. Lewis says that Charn's later rulers had "done dreadful things and also suffered dreadful things." The mark of the magician is on them. For the knowledge that established their position of power, they put down the human part of themselves, until human pleasures were no longer possible for them.

Jadis is a worthy descendant of this cruel and powerful house. She is very tall, beautiful, proud, strong, brave, cunning, ruthless, and practical. She speaks to no one but the person she wants to make use of. She does not even see anyone else. In Charn, she latches on to Digory and ignores Polly. In England, she fixes on Uncle Andrew and forgets the children. Her story shows the depraved state to which Charn has come in its latter days. As they walk through the palace, Jadis points out the principal landmarks, which are all characterized by horrible deeds that have occurred there in centuries past.

As Jadis describes it, Charn's history was reduced in the end to a struggle over which of two ruthless sisters would rule the world. They first fought a conventional war, which Jadis's sister won, that destroyed all of Jadis's armies. Then when her sister was ready to claim victory, Jadis resorted to the Deplorable Word, which wiped out all living things except herself. The analogy to nuclear weapons is obvious. Lewis is saying that if an all-out war were to be fought, the participants might try to avoid the use of nuclear weapons. But in the end, with one side ready to wipe out the other, the choice would be made to eliminate all living things rather than knuckle under to a hated rival. All witches would like to know the Deplorable Word. They don't really care whether anything other than themselves grows and thrives. And every witch, given enough power, would eventually destroy everything else or make everyone else a slave, as the house of Charn has done in that world.

Though they are so different in power and courage, Jadis and Uncle Andrew are alike in other respects. Neither cares for anyone's well-being except his or her own. Both are horribly practical in being insensitive to the beauty and joy of life and aware only of people and circumstances which will forward their goals. Both believe that others exist to serve them. Jadis feels she is being magnanimous in offering her sister peace in subjection, even though she has made the river of Charn run red with the blood of her armies. Both have paid dearly for their horrible knowledge. Andrew's hair has turned gray, and Jadis has paid a terrible price to learn the Deplorable Word. And both have that mark of wickedness about them, that feeling of malevolence, which should warn casual bystanders to stay away if they value their lives.

But even her power and occult knowledge cannot keep Jadis from making a fool of herself. When Digory tells her his Uncle Andrew has sent them to Charn, Jadis creates a grandiose fiction about his being the great king of this earth and sending Digory and Polly to fetch her because he has learned of her great beauty. She flies into a rage when Polly tells her this is "absolute bosh." Jadis makes the same mistake later on when the crowd jeeringly cheers for "the Hempress of Colney 'Atch." She bows slightly to this supposed praise, until she learns they are making fun of her. Then, again in a rage, she strikes out at every policeman in sight. Her vanity is more awesome but no less ridiculous than that of Uncle Andrew—who tries to impress his "visitor" by wearing his best suit and screwing in his monocle.

Jadis in England is pure comedy. In Charn, she might be able to fool the listener into thinking she really is as noble as she says she is. In London, when stripped of her powers, she is nothing but another outlaw. She is exposed as a common burglar, boor, roughneck, animal abuser, and attempted assassin. You have to admire Aunt Letty for standing up to the shameless but imposing person with the bare arms. It is less hazardous to stand up to evil and be brushed aside than to follow along meekly like Uncle Andrew and lose your watch and chain and your self-respect, as well as your virtue.

Just as England exposes the myth of nobility in Jadis, the new land of Narnia reveals Uncle Andrew as a cowardly, two-bit entrepreneur. But he receives his comeuppance from the land he wishes to exploit and the animals he wishes to eliminate. He whines the whole time they are there and is nicknamed *Brandy* because of his constant calls for that beverage. He persistently tries to maneuver Digory away from the others and persuade him to put on his green ring so that they can return home. He doesn't even know the green ring is the wrong one to use. The only things about Narnia that really interest Uncle Andrew are the good air and the growability of everything in the young soil. When he sees the lamp-post growing, he can envision reaping huge profits from the interworld transport of scrap iron to Narnia and finished products back to earth.

Uncle Andrew's visit to Narnia is an exercise in self-deception. He hears Aslan singing a new world into existence, but he does not like the song. In addition, his common sense tells him that lions can't sing. So he gradually convinces himself that the lion is only roaring. After a great deal of effort, not only has he convinced himself that Aslan and the other beasts are only making their characteristic noises, but, in fact, all he can hear is roaring, barking, yelping, and other sounds. As Lewis succinctly put it, "The trouble about trying to make yourself stupider than you are is that you very often succeed." His successful effort cuts him off from effective communication with the inhabitants of Narnia. The results are comic but appropriate. Since he will not treat the talking animals as rational creatures, they do not recognize him as one. So they plant him as a tree.

The world is full of Uncle Andrews, in the form of people who are shrewd operators in terms of protecting their own short-term interests, but are blind to everything truly meaningful in life. They are always looking for an angle—a way to beat the system. They grow poor, looking for a shortcut to wealth. When they come in contact with life's ultimate realities, they play games with their minds until the Lord can no longer speak to them. They are convinced that evangelists are just like them: people playing a religious angle to get others on their side. They can see nothing particularly successful or worth emulating in Jesus' life. So they go about their business, cheating themselves and others, until life becomes a dreary path toward a friendless death.

Jadis's reaction to Narnia is even stronger than Uncle Andrew's. She hates everything about it, and she especially hates Aslan. She instinctively recognizes that here is a power stronger than hers, and she can tolerate no competition. She is just as eager as Uncle Andrew to get out of Narnia and hates him for trying to leave without her. But her response to Aslan's song is more courageous than her fellow magician's. She tries to attack Aslan with the bar she has wrenched from the lamp-post. When it has no effect on him, even the fearless Jadis flees in terror.

Jadis does not offer the same opportunity for evangelism that Uncle Andrew does. He seems a hard case, but he has not finally closed the only door to escape from himself. A pure life might become an effective testimony to Uncle Andrew. Jadis has closed the door. She is confirmed in evil. Realizing that there is a good stronger than her evil does not make her repent. It only increases her hatred and desire for revenge. She will fight the despised lion as long as she can. When she is defeated, she will die cursing him. Like Satan, there is no hope but that of frustrating the good as long and as effectively as possible.

There are people like Jadis in this world. They are not as numerous as the Uncle Andrews, but they are there. If a man faces them without God, they will use him mercilessly for their own purposes and then cast him aside. If a man has any exposed weaknesses, Satan will be sure to work through his people in exploiting them. The believer will not always be able to distinguish between a Jadis and an Uncle Andrew, and he does not need to. He need only maintain a close relationship with God, who alone is stronger than any foe, and try to present a consistent testimony to all men and women. If one is completely at His disposal, he shall find in the end that a few Uncle Andrews have been influenced in the Lord's direction by his testimony and that the Jadises in his life threaten but do not vanquish him.

The Calm before Creation

Although the occult receives much attention in *The Magician's Nephew*, the book is also devoted to a study of life: the various forms life can take, the beginning of life, the source of life, the protection of life, and the recovery of life. Life begins in the brand-new land of Narnia and ends in the worn-out world of Charn. Life ripples over the landscape like a green wave and bursts out in myriad forms. But whenever life manifests itself, it always has one source, and that source is God.

C. S. Lewis may have intended the Wood between the Worlds to be a pictorial representation of the mind of God. Lewis says that as Polly and Digory approach the Wood, they pass from darkness into a soft green light that makes Digory think he is underwater, until finally they burst through the surface of a pool into that quiet place. Man's form of existence must look, from God's point of view, as if he is underwater. Compared to God's vitality and awareness, it must appear that man is almost asleep—walking through the darkness created by earthly sin.

As a man turns from his knowledge to God's concerns, the light of God's Word begins to shine on him. He begins to understand God—first in a limited fashion, but with ever-increasing depth—until, like Digory, he bursts through into the center of God's thoughts, where everything is calm and peaceful and rich and growing. His mind no longer seems to be underwater.

Even when Polly and Digory arrive at the Wood between the Worlds, they are not quite at the core of life. The trees of that Wood are so leafy that no direct sunlight filters through. Only an indirect green light can penetrate the leaves. But that light is so bright and warm that it must have been produced by a very strong sun.

As Cleland B. McAfee writes in a hymn:

> There is a place of quiet rest,
> Near to the heart of God,
> A place where sin cannot molest,
> Near to the heart of God.

Lewis paints a picture of that place: It is very still and peaceful. There are no animals there except one misdirected guinea pig. It is filled only with trees and leaves and innumerable pools and sod and green daylight, yet it is not dull. Although the only activity is the growing of the trees, Digory tells us the Wood is "as rich as plumcake" and very much alive. It is not the sort of place where things happen. It is, instead, the entry point to all the places where things happen. Digory compares it to the tunnel next to the attic that runs through Polly's house and all the adjoining ones. Nothing happens there, but you can go from this in-between place into any house on the block.

God's mind is like that. There is a stillness at the core of His being—a place where activity ceases. Thought and caring and vitality are present, but there is not a frenzy of doing. God invites man to be quiet with Him, to put aside pressing concerns, and be still and know that He is God. For a moment Polly and Digory forget the great adventure they are engaged in. This is not a rest that creates ennui, as does repetitious, meaningless action.

If this sounds like a commercial for daily devotions, it is. People often wonder what Jesus did during all those hours alone in the wilderness and up in the mountains. He told His disciples He was communing with His Father, and Lewis's Wood between the Worlds is a picture of that communion. But instead of yellow rings, the vehicle that takes men straight to the Father is prayer.

The presence of God is life to those who love Him, but it is death to those who turn away from His will. That is why Jadis is stifled during her few moments in the Wood between the Worlds. She has chosen long ago to put God behind her and to focus all her attention on the expansion of her own ego. Everything about God is hateful to her, because He possesses power greater than hers, and she cannot stand to have anyone else above her. The stagnation of Charn suits her much more than the green Wood, because she has put all Charn under her feet. She has made it unlivable in the process, but that is a secondary concern. She simply decides to take her act to some other world, where there are other subjects to conquer.

When Jadis leaves the Wood between the Worlds, she forgets she has ever been there! Her mind simply cannot comprehend God's thoughts, so she puts them out of her head. His perspective shows her for what she is: an absurdity.

The Lion's Song

The quiet of the Wood between the Worlds also represents the calm before creation. All activity begins in the mind of God. Before the worlds were, He was; and His thoughts have called them into being. It is appropriate to visit the Wood between the Worlds and then witness the creation of a world.

The creation of Narnia is full of insight into how this world may have come into being. Lewis does not pretend to re-create the day the world began exactly as it happened. There are differences between the narrative in *The Magician's Nephew* and the biblical account, but in an important sense, Lewis's book fleshes out the record of the first two chapters of Genesis.

Lewis begins by describing the nothing that precedes creation. Jadis is the first to really understand that they are in an empty world. She cannot comprehend the Wood between the Worlds, but she can relate to the void. That, in a sense, is where she lives. Cut off from God and her fellow creatures, she may surround herself with jewels and gorgeous accouterments, but she is essentially living in a vacuum.

Some creation has already taken place in Narnia before the visitors arrive. The creation of the firmament and the gathering of waters into one place, which Moses says occurred on the second day, have already happened in Narnia. This was necessary for the party from earth and Charn to have a place to stand to watch the spectacle. But there is no light yet, and the sensation of darkness is exactly like the inside of a cave, where one can see absolutely nothing.

This is the scene in which Aslan, the great lion, begins singing his song of creation. Lewis describes this activity as a song, but the Genesis account refers only to God speaking. But Job 38:7 mentions, in connection with the creation, the time when the morning stars sang together. The first things created by Aslan's song are stars. Thus Lewis combines the light, created on the first day in Genesis, with the stars, created on the fourth. Not only does Aslan sing the stars into being, but they sing back in response. The fact is that everything positive a man can do is a response to something God has first done for him, beginning with birth.

Lewis makes a point of the fact that everything that is being created is coming right out of the lion's head. This is creativity in its purest sense. When God created the heavens and the earth, everything that came into being literally came out of His head. It was not a spur-of-the-moment thing, since all creation, history, and redemption were foreknown by God. But as John reminds us, "Apart from Him nothing came into being that has come into being" (John 1:3 NASB). After creation of the stars, Aslan sings the sun into existence, completing the events that parallel Moses's fourth day. Then Aslan changes his tune, a carpet of green spreads out from him, and grass, heather, trees, flowers, and other vegetation come into being; and Moses's third day of creation is completed. Lumps appear under the new green surface of the land, and these swell and burst into animals, paralleling events of Moses's fifth and sixth days. Lewis's description of Aslan breathing the breath of life into those creatures selected to be talking animals is very similar to the biblical record of God breathing life into Adam and Eve.

This event again emphasizes the reality and importance of the living soul. Without souls, men are just perishable beasts. With them, they are eternal beings capable of knowing God on the most intimate level. Aslan especially wants the talking animals not to forget themselves and emulate the dumb beasts that are in subjection to them. Man's physical form may not change if he ignores his soulish nature, but inwardly his actions may become more and more bestial until, like the witch, his mind does not even remember that he has been in the presence of God, and he at last finds himself in the void.

One of the instructive effects of Aslan's song is what it does to the London cabby. His life in the big city has made him sharp and quarrelsome and quick to speak. Now that he is back in what is, for him, a more natural environment, his mannerisms begin to change. He is slower and more deliberate, and he seems braver and kinder. He, more than any of the others, realizes the power and beauty of what Aslan is doing. He ridicules Uncle Andrew's suggestion that Aslan could be shot, and he keeps shushing the others so he can listen to the "moosic."

When Aslan ask the cabby to become king of the new land, he feels inadequate but agrees to do each of the things Aslan says is required of a king. The list clears up the misconceptions Uncle Andrew seems to have about what the role of a general or other leader is. Frank must be willing to till the earth along with his subjects; being a worker as well as a supervisor is important. He must rule the talking animals as free subjects and not slaves. They have minds of their own, and as long as they contribute to the general welfare of the realm and do not abuse their neighbors, they should not be constrained to act contrary to their wishes. He must not play favorites and must not let any of his subjects harass or wrongfully use their fellow creatures. He must be in the forefront in meeting any danger that comes against the land.

The Apple of Life

Throughout *The Magician's Nephew*, Digory is depressed because his mother seems fatally ill. He is very sensitive to comments others make about her. Uncle Andrew uses her twice as a means of making Digory be quiet and do what his uncle suggests. And Digory is always on the lookout for anything that might help her or restore her health. That is why he becomes very excited when he overhears his aunt saying that nothing will help his mother except fruit from the land of youth. Since he knows there are other worlds, he has high hopes that he may be able to find the land of youth, where such fruit grows. This hope is reinforced when Uncle Andrew says Narnia is the land of youth. Uncle Andrew cares nothing about Digory's mother, but the chance of a miraculous cure seems more and more likely to Digory.

Finally, he gathers the courage to speak to Aslan about it. He is much chagrined when Aslan changes the subject and asks him why he has brought a powerful witch into the new and unspoiled land of Narnia. Digory considers evading the issue, but he wisely decides to confess that his insatiable curiosity and pride have brought this evil into Narnia. When he has made his confession, he is sure there is no chance for his mother. After Aslan asks Digory if he is ready to remedy the evil, Digory considers promising to do so only if his mother is restored. But he realizes, just in time, that one does not bargain with Aslan. At last, in desperation, Digory pleads for his mother. He is amazed to discover by Aslan's tears that the lion cares about her even more than her own son does.

So far, Digory's story is another example of the sinner saved by grace. Every one of the Narnia books contains such a story. Like Shasta in *The Horse and His Boy* and Trumpkin in *Prince Caspian*, Digory does not seem to have a bad character. But he does have a flaw that causes a great deal of grief to those around him. Digory's sin is wanting to know too much. He is so eager to visit another world that he almost loses his way of escape back to his own world. He cannot bear to leave the little golden bell unstruck. And he cannot wait to know if Aslan will help his mother. Aslan deliberately frustrates this demand to know by sending Digory off on an errand that must be fulfilled before any more questions are asked.

Digory represents the modern demand for instant information. Lewis favored deep knowledge to that which is wide but superficial. In order to be valuable, knowledge of what is going on in the world must lead to a gain in understanding and patience. God's timetable will not lead to man's running around in frenzied activity to accomplish his desires. Likewise, His timing cannot be rushed.

At first Digory feels that Aslan is uncaring about his mother, but he learns that Aslan cares more about her than he does. Likewise, Jesus' tears show more compassion than those of the dead Lazarus's two sisters, Mary and Martha. God is never cold and unfeeling. He may not take what a man considers the direct route in solving the problems of those He loves, but His wisdom is always in control of His compassion. And He does not care for the needs of one of His children by neglecting the needs of another.

When Digory receives his commission, the story begins to take on another cast. Up to this point it has been a tale of personal error, confession, and repentance. When he rides toward the Western Wild on Fledge's back, Digory represents the whole nation of Narnia in an interesting reenactment of the early days of this world. The magical tree set in a walled garden toward which he rides is strongly reminiscent of both the tree of the knowledge of good and evil and the tree of life in the Garden of Eden. Lewis describes what would have happened if Adam and Eve had eaten of the tree of life before they were evicted from the Garden.

Digory approaches the garden through golden gates, which are straight from the tenth chapter of John: "Truly, truly, I say to you, he who does not enter by the door into the fold of the sheep, but climbs up some other way, he is a thief and a robber. But he who enters by the door is a shepherd of the sheep. . . . I am the door; if anyone enters through Me, he will be saved, and will go in and out and find pasture" (John 10:1–2, 9 NASB). The thief in this garden, as well as the deceitful snake, is Jadis. She has not entered into the garden by the gates, which represent the way of salvation. But she has made her own way over the wall and misappropriated the fruit of the tree for her own use. She tries to get Digory to do the same.

The words on the golden gates say, "Those who steal or those who climb my wall shall find their heart's desire and find despair." As the witch tempts him, he has exactly the same choice Adam and Eve had to make. Aside from the fact that it has been forbidden, he can see no reason not to enjoy an apple from the tree. and the verse itself might be construed to condone taking an apple for his mother. Besides, just as Eve could see "that the tree was good for food, and that it was a delight to the eyes, and that the tree was desirable to make one wise" (Gen. 3:6 NASB), so Digory is overcome by the pure deliciousness of the smell of the apple.

The witch plays on his love for his mother, as well as his desire for power. She tells him how easy it would be to restore her to health. The fact that his mother herself would disapprove of stealing and breaking promises is a deterrent. But the thing that finally decides him against Adam and Eve's mistake is a tactical error by the witch: She tells him he can leave Polly behind, and he suddenly sees through her scheme, which is to leave Narnia vulnerable to her power.

When he successfully completes his mission, Aslan tells him how close he has come to calamity. Aslan informs Digory that "things always work according to their nature." By eating the apple at the wrong time, unbidden, Jadis "has won her heart's desire; she has unwearying strength and endless days like a goddess. But length of days with an evil heart is only length of misery and already she begins to know it. All get what they want: they do not always like it."

The mysteries of sin and hell are contained in these words. Eating the forbidden apple has turned Jadis as white as salt—a whiteness that comes from knowing she will live forever but have no joy. That, in fact, is what hell is all about. It is a continuous state of misery that a man brings on himself by insisting on his own way. Very often sin is not a matter of doing something positively bad. It is sometimes a matter of doing something right at the wrong time or in the wrong way.

God was anxious to get Adam and Eve out of the Garden of Eden because if they had eaten of the tree of life, they would have been doomed to the hopeless longevity suffered by Jadis. God had another plan. He means eventually to bring back the tree of life (which He foretells in Revelation 22:2), but there is much that must happen first. He does not just want man to have eternal existence. Instead, He desires man to have eternal life—real life, full of the joy of fellowship and fulfillment. To experience salvation, many must first enter into the straight and narrow way that leads to life, by entering the gate that lies beyond the shed blood of Christ. Man's efforts are fruitless; His gracious provision alone is sufficient. One need not struggle to go through that gate; it opens to the touch. If a man refuses that door, he will find there is no other. All who are in hell choose to find a shortcut.

The consequence of Digory's refusing to take a shortcut to get the apple of life for his mother is that he can go later, with Aslan's blessing. That makes the difference between a blessed and a cursed event. Aslan tells Digory that he and his mother would live to rue the day that he acted on his own to save her. God will not always do exactly what man thinks He should do. Sometimes the loved one will die. But every setback gives the believer the opportunity for a new exercise of faith. Man cannot always see with God's eyes, but he can always trust in His wisdom. And sometimes, beyond hope, the thing he wishes for most will happen. In fact, as the Christian draws closer to God, he will find himself more often desiring the event that turns out to be God's will.

2

The Lion, the Witch
and the Wardrobe

The Lion, the Witch and the Wardrobe begins the Pevensie children's excursion into Narnia and tells an allegorical tale of the death and resurrection of Christ. Beyond the obvious plane of the story line is a wealth of Christian symbolism and imagery.

Allegory and Symbolism

Determining the precise significance of a book's imagery is always a difficult task, particularly when you deal with an author like C. S. Lewis. Unlike the medieval fantasizers, Lewis usually avoided sustained allegory in his writings. Yet, unlike his friend J. R. R. Tolkien, Lewis did not completely scorn the use of allegory. His first book, *The Pilgrim's Regress*, is a true allegory, but the Narnia chronicles contain a mixture of symbolism and passages that are pure fantasy, without profound meaning.

In *The Lion, the Witch and the Wardrobe*, the lion and the witch are obvious symbols, although they are more than that, as well. Each has life apart from symbolic significance. The White Witch has all the characteristics of a witch, and Aslan is very feline and ferocious. Other characters form a natural place in the fantasy world being created but are not intentional symbols. The faun introduced in chapter one is a good example. Other sources say that Lewis did not introduce the faun to give the book more meaning. In fact, it was quite the other way around. The image of a faun hurrying through snowy woods, carrying an umbrella and a pile of packages, came to Lewis one day. He started thinking about how to work the image into a story, and the Narnia books were the result. Lewis loved fantasy for its own sake, and the richness of Narnia provides ample evidence to the power of his imagination.

In chapter one, Lewis uses patterns familiar to all readers of fairy tales, but he shows once again that, when used skillfully, old formulas can always be given new life. He introduces the four main characters and brings them to an old house, full of rooms, mystery, and the likelihood of adventure. That ancient structure represents the way the world looks to a child: Very little is known; much is new and unexplored; much seems threatening; and yet everything is old in comparison to the child.

The wardrobe introduces a concept that will be emphasized frequently in the Narnia books: The inside is bigger than the outside. From the outside, the wardrobe appears very ordinary. It is a known quantity, even to the children. However, inside, Lucy finds much more than she expects to. She is drawn by the soft feel of warm fur, only to find a second row of coats and to be drawn farther into what turns out to be Narnia. Lewis makes a beautiful transition between England and Narnia. The crunch of snow under one's feet does indeed feel and sound like the crunch of mothballs, and one can imagine soft fur changing gradually into evergreen needles. The image of the faun completes the transition from the mundane to a very vivid world of fantasy.

Fantasy is never hazy or unreal in Lewis's books. It is a concrete, tangible thing that, for a time, is more real than the everyday world. Lewis purposely avoided a technique often used to introduce fantasies: the dream. Putting fantasy into a dream would make it appear strictly an inner psychological phenomenon used only to escape from reality, and Lewis does not want to create this impression. To him, fantasy, or the reality of which fantasy speaks, existed outside his mind. He did not so much generate the Narnia world as he discovered it. It exists out there, to be apprehended by anyone with sufficient sensitivity.

Much of Lewis's philosophy rests on the concept that the inside is bigger than the outside. He felt that the great weakness of the twentieth century is its mania for debunking—its tendency to reduce all phenomena to their lowest physical or physiological bases. Thus, Freudian philosophers tend to attribute all motivation to purely animal desires; logical positivists do not believe anything that can't be seen; moralists condone any behavior that seems comfortable or nondestructive under the circumstances; and Christian existentialists believe in God, while believing that their belief is impossible.

Lewis hated this philosophy with a passion. He affirmed the reality of ideas as strongly as Plato ever did. One of the most dramatic moments in *That Hideous Strength* occurs when Mark Studdock is placed in a room calculated to teach perversion. Everything is slightly off. The pictures, most of which portray ordinary or religious scenes, contain too much dirt and too many beetles. The walls are misaligned. A group of dots on the ceiling is not quite arranged in a symmetrical fashion. But, on Mark, the room creates the opposite effect of what was intended. All the asymmetry around him helps create in his mind an idea of the normal, the straight, the properly proportioned. These ideas grow to the size of mountains within him and give him something to rest on and take hold of.

In an essay published in *God in the Dock*, Lewis says that one must look *along* things as well as look at them, in order to achieve full understanding. One cannot know music or art or pain or love or God by looking at them objectively, unless he also enters into a subjective experience of their essence. Something that is quite common and small when looked at may be extraordinary and large when experienced. Even an ordinary wardrobe might contain the world of Narnia.

The Children as Disciples

It is tempting to cast the children in the role of disciples, particularly in the light of their relationship with Aslan. There is, of course, no one-to-one identification between Lucy, Edmund, Susan, and Peter and Christ's original disciples, but there are similarities. These become clearer in the books that follow; but even in the children's first adventure in Narnia, characteristic traits begin to emerge.

Peter deserves the role of the apostle Paul. At first he doesn't seem much like Paul at all. He doesn't have that ranting, persecuting, firebrand personality that may be attributed to the unregenerate Paul. Peter is more similar to the converted Paul, the leader of the Gentile church. Paul possessed the mind that God used to explain the truth behind the events recorded in the Gospels and Acts.

Peter, too, because of his age and ability, is acknowledged as the leader. He begins by sincerely failing to realize that Lucy is telling the truth about Narnia. He is very kind to her, but the fact that he obviously thinks she is lying or demented must have wounded her more than Edmund's ill-natured barbs. Peter's ignorance is, in fact, a form of persecution for Lucy. When Peter finds out the truth, he quickly asserts his leadership in Narnia and is the first to work out the logical implications of their adventures. To give Lucy her due, she often feels the truth before Peter can recognize it, but she never challenges his leadership.

Lucy is much like John, the disciple whom Jesus loved. Her love for Narnia and Aslan is immediate, spontaneous, and unshakable. The strangeness of the new world does not cause her to lose her bearings (although she is a bit frightened), because she has an inner monitor that reacts to the realities of things rather than their appearances. Her ability to penetrate the surface is reminiscent of Frodo's reaction to Strider in J. R. R. Tolkien's *Lord of the Rings*; Strider's ranger outfit and weathered aspect do not impress Frodo, but he recognizes that Strider is someone who can be trusted. The contrast to Edmund, who can see in the White Witch only a source of endless Turkish Delight, is obvious.

Edmund is a bit harder to categorize. For a long time, he seems to be Judas, betraying his companions at every turn. But he does come around in the end, rather in the fashion of the apostle Peter. Peter makes every mistake in the book, until he receives his spiritual baptism at Pentecost, though his denial of Christ prior to the crucifixion provides the most obvious parallel to Edmund's experience. As Lewis says, one of the nastiest things Edmund ever did was denying the reality of Narnia after being there with Lucy. Christ must have felt some of the same emotion that Lucy expresses when she bolts from the room, crying.

Susan does not really show her true colors in this book. She seems the soul of sensibility and compromise, a girl who generally displays a cool, mature manner.

The Old House

A number of recorders of the world of fantasy, including George MacDonald, develop the idea that certain places on this earth are much more susceptible than others to strange happenings; they are, if you will, doors and windows into the mysterious. The professor's house is such a place. But it is more than just a source of mystery; it is a house of opportunity and destiny. In this book that destiny is focused on an old wardrobe. True to its nature, mystery cannot be invoked at one's discretion. The wardrobe is not an automatic door to Narnia. It can provide transit between the two worlds only at the destined times. When the four children enter Narnia, they do so not because they have chosen it, but because they are escaping from the Macready and are, in effect, harried into Narnia.

Psalm 2 affirms the paradox that God makes the wrath of man to please Him. This passage contains the crux of the dilemma about human volition and divine ordination. Man is really free to choose (at least in the ultimate sense of following God or Satan), but his choices are made to fit into God's overall plan. Mysterious places—situations where a narrow, mundane existence suddenly expands with the possibility of new life and meaning—are one of the ways God uses to make this paradox come true. In the midst of sinning and struggling and straying, man suddenly hits an intersection—a point where the aimless line of his life meets God's direction. At that moment, and at that moment only, he decides whether to plunge straight ahead into oblivion or to allow the liberation of God's guidance.

This point is given force by the relationship between Narnia time and earth time. One can never be sure how much earth time, if any, will have elapsed while one has been traveling in Narnia. The children's adventure in Narnia is, in effect, an expansion of one key moment in their lives. They are given the opportunity of choosing and learning and growing. Their experience seems to them and to us to take a long time, but this is not actually the case. Profound changes, at least in direction, really can occur during brief periods of time.

The Great Lion

The presence of Aslan broods over Narnia like a pervasive, loving, but rather frightening spirit. He is, however, very much a flesh-and-blood lion. Lewis gives a vivid picture of what the incarnation of Christ would be like were it to occur in a world dominated by animals with living souls and reason. If Aslan had been a man, the parallel with this world would have been too close, and the reader would have labored to distinguish the historical Christ of the Bible from the imaginative one of Lewis's creation. Because he is depicted as an animal, Aslan does not compete with Christ; he illumines Him. The Narnia books show Christ much as the first century saw Him—with the freshness and bloom of first encounter and stripped of the banalities that have grown up around the Lord of glory.

The Pevensie children get their first real description of Aslan in the home of the Beavers. Mr. Beaver describes Aslan as something of an absentee landlord: He is lord of the wood but is not often physically present. Aslan most often works in Narnia through those who are faithful to him, such as the Beavers. There is no question in Mr. Beaver's mind whether Aslan or the White Witch is the most powerful. Although he has never seen Aslan and has spent his whole life in the frigidity of the White Witch's winter, Aslan is a spiritual reality to him. He knows the witch is a local tyrant, while Aslan is the king, the son of the great Emperor-Beyond-the-Sea, with the power to put local tyrants in their places. "If she can stand on her two feet and look him in the face it'll be the most she can do and more than I expect of her!" Lewis knows that in the final analysis Satan is a coward and will avoid a direct confrontation with divine purpose.

Lewis makes fascinating use of terminology that is only casual or mythical in our world. When Mr. Beaver says that Aslan, the great lion, is the king of beasts, he literally means it. Similarly, the creatures that Lewis draws from Greek and Roman mythology, such as fauns, satyrs, centaurs, dryads, and naiads, are pictured as a normal part of the Narnian world. It seems as if Lewis is saying that creatures and stories that are fantastic in our world may have some relation to reality in some other world—that fantasy and myth contain valid principles that are important even in the everyday struggle for existence. Lewis once remarked that the proportion of sense to total verbiage varies from almost 60 percent in children's books to practically nothing in social-science textbooks.

Lewis especially emphasizes the point that Aslan is both good and terrible (in the sense of being terrifying). He is not a tame lion. The Beavers think it ridiculous that Susan and Lucy expect him to be safe. When the children first meet him, they are overcome by the sight of "the golden mane and the great, royal, solemn, overwhelming eyes." Lucy realizes that he has "terrible paws . . . if he didn't know how to velvet them!" And they are not always velveted. When Aslan and the White Witch consummate their arrangements for delivering Edmund from death, she questions whether or not Aslan will keep his promise. His response is to let out a roar so frightening that she must run for her life. Even when he is in a playful mood, Lucy can never quite decide whether their romp is "more like playing with a thunderstorm or playing with a kitten."

Peter strikes the right note when he says, "I'm longing to see him . . . even if I do feel frightened when it comes to the point." Peter's standing before Aslan is comparable to a man standing before Christ. It will not be comfortable to stand before the Lord with all of one's past thoughts and deeds exposed.

Lewis makes it very clear that Aslan is a real lion, just as Christ is shown as being very human in the Bible. Aslan roars at the witch when she questions his integrity. He roars for pure joy after his resurrection from the dead. But he is every inch a great cat in his mad romp with Susan and Lucy on the hill of the Stone Table. They see him with "his eyes very bright, his limbs quivering, lashing himself with his tail."

Even after his resurrection, however, Aslan's chief joy is in delivering his followers. In the courtyard of the witch's castle, he is whisking around like "a cat chasing its tail," breathing on creatures the witch had turned to stone and reviving them. He is not even afraid to acknowledge his kinship with other lions. A stone lion brought back to life goes wild with joy when Aslan refers to "us lions." But the lion still is not foolish enough to confuse himself with Aslan, the king of beasts. The kinship of man with Christ should be a source of great humility as well as deep joy.

Aslan's effect on the children, his disciples, is as remarkable as he is. Like Jesus, he has only a short time to be with them and prepare them for his death and their duties. Peter cannot understand why Aslan is showing him how to conduct the battle against the witch; he does not realize the price Aslan will have to pay to free Edmund. Nevertheless, Aslan's presence with the children is like a refreshing oasis. After their romp with him, Susan and Lucy "no longer felt in the least tired or hungry or thirsty."

Perhaps a picture of how the Holy Spirit intends to lead and sustain the believer is in the thrilling ride Susan and Lucy take on Aslan's back from the hill of the Stone

Table to the witch's castle. They fly through the forest "about twice as fast as the fastest racehorse" on "a mount that doesn't need to be guided and never grows tired." Aslan takes them right over the castle wall into the witch's courtyard, where dead statues are made to live. With the Holy Spirit in control, not even the gates of hell will prevail against the Christian.

Sin and Evil

After considering the splendor of Aslan, it is almost painful to begin a discussion of sin and evil as Lewis portrays them. The world has a tendency to think of evil as mysterious and interesting, and good as bland and boring. In Narnia, the reverse is really true. Aslan is mysterious and exciting, while the witch is cruel but colorless. As Lewis knew from his study of Saint Augustine, sin and evil have no existence of their own, but are only parasites on good. Sin, or perversity, is turning from what is right, and evil, or depravity, is the absence of virtue that results.

Edmund is a perfect example of perverse sin leading to depraved evil. Early in the book, he comes under the influence of the White Witch. She bribes him with, of all things, Turkish Delight. When one thinks of someone selling his soul to the devil, he usually thinks of Faust, who obtained years of riotous pleasure and immense wealth in exchange. Actually, most people sell themselves much cheaper than that. Even Turkish Delight might do the trick. Of course, part of man's pleasure in sinning comes from the sense that he's getting away with something. What he usually fails to realize is the effect that his sins have on him. Mr. Beaver notices right away that Edmund has been eating the witch's food. Edmund feels misused by the others, especially Peter, and even his judgment is distorted. He thinks that his patroness, the witch, can turn Aslan into stone. Lewis says that "the mention of Aslan gave him a mysterious and horrible feeling just as it gave the others a mysterious and lovely feeling." Edmund doesn't realize it yet, but he is cutting himself off from the one being who can really make him happy.

Edmund's journey from Beaversdam to the witch's castle is a picture of the sin-induced slide into evil. Step-by-step, he becomes more and more confused, wrong-headed, bitter, and unhappy. He had not enjoyed dinner at the Beavers, because, as Lewis says, "there's nothing that spoils the taste of good ordinary food half so much as the memory of bad magic food." So many lives have been wrecked because people abandon the real pleasures they possess for the lure of something new that, if attained, will not bring happiness or satisfaction.

On his trudge through snowy, dark woods, Edmund nourishes his grievances. He is sustained by his hatred of Peter and the hope of becoming king of Narnia. He even rationalizes that the witch is not as bad as everyone says. He reflects that she was nice to him. Gratification of personal, selfish desires has become more important than the safety and welfare of others. He even plans what he will do when he becomes king and decides to bring modern technological improvements to Narnia. He fails to realize the absurdity of streets and cinemas in a world made for animals. Lewis was no friend of progress for progress's sake. In his science fiction books, he takes numerous potshots at those who insist upon the claims of technology, regardless of morality or good judgment.

When he reaches the witch's castle, Edmund is momentarily frightened by a lion that has been turned into a statue. After discovering that it is only stone, he feels very brave, defaces the lion, and even talks himself into thinking that the witch has turned Aslan into stone. This whole episode exemplifies the world's attitude toward Christianity. People do not usually reject real Christianity; they reject a caricature of it. The church is ridiculed because it is full of hypocrites; the Bible, which most have never read, is cast aside because of its alleged contradictions. The Christian's God is mocked because He does not eliminate evil and suffering, although to do so would be to destroy free will.

Lewis himself was raised in a church that taught him the fear of hell but not the reality of Christ. He turned from what he thought was a lifeless statue to atheism. But he finally discovered the thrill of true Christianity in the works of George MacDonald and others. As Lewis once said, a young atheist can never be too careful of his reading. It turned out that real excitement was only to be discovered in the works of Christians, not atheists.

When Edmund finishes his journey into darkness, he receives his reward: Turkish Delight in the form of stale bread and water. Edmund is a victim of the law of diminishing returns. What seemed so delicious when first encountered leads, in the end, to an unpalatable reality. Satan uses this technique with great effect. He gives men a little bit of pleasure with the promise of a great deal more if they will only lower their standards, cheat, bend the rules, and otherwise violate God's laws. When they do, the reward is as distasteful as Edmund's. Isaiah's question is pertinent: "Why do you spend your money for that which is not bread, and your labor for that which does not satisfy?" (Isa. 55:2).

Just as Edmund represents man's progression into sin, the White Witch represents the end of the journey for a creature confirmed in evil. The result of her way of life is not pretty. The contrast between good and evil is clear when she is seen next to Aslan. His golden face is full of life, while her dead-white face is monotonous in its cruelty and hatred and obsession with power. Narnia in the grip of the White Witch's winter is sterile and uninteresting. Nothing exciting ever happens; it is always winter but never Christmas. The very whiteness of her realm is oppressive. Her face symbolizes life with the sap drawn out of it. Lewis tells us, "Her face was white—not merely pale, but white like snow or paper or icing sugar." Here is the antiseptic purity of evil.

Mr. Beaver describes the witch as being not really human, though she pretends to be. He goes on to say that you should be suspicious of anything that pretends to be human and is not or used to be human and is not. The idea is that goodness has a way of becoming more and more itself, while evil is always covering up what it is or masquerading as something else.

Evil does have its moments of triumph, but they are short-lived. There is a look of fierce joy on the witch's face when she makes her pact with Aslan. She believes that she has really won. But while the ways of righteousness may appear to be stupid and unproductive, looks are often deceiving. The witch thinks Aslan a fool for agreeing to die for Edmund; she even intends to renege on the bargain when Aslan is dead and kill her enemies anyway. What she fails to realize is that her actions and Aslan's death have been foreseen and are a part of a plan. Death is swallowed up in victory, and a season of evil becomes a season of good.

Sacrifice and Salvation

Aslan's death and resurrection are the pivotal events of *The Lion, the Witch and the Wardrobe* and invite comparison with the biblical account. This is the most symbolic portion of the Narnia books. Lewis uses the Christian concepts of sin and salvation, but in order to have a believable narrative, he avoids remaining too near the biblical account. By making his story parallel the biblical account, without following it exactly, he invites comparison without causing confusion. Narnia is different from this world, and its salvation story must reflect it. Aslan's experience varies just enough to shed new light on the agony of Christ.

An integral part of salvation is that sin deserves death. When the children discover that Edmund has committed a sin, and therefore deserves death, Lucy asks whether Aslan can save him. Aslan responds, "All shall be done. . . . But it may be harder than you think." She does not realize that Aslan's life is the price. Likewise, Jesus' disciples did not understand that He had to die, although He told them so several times; they thought He could save them by destroying their enemies.

But sin, whether in Narnia or in our world, is paid wages: death. The witch knows enough to demand a body, and she gets one. She even recites the Narnian equivalent of Scripture: the magic written on the Stone Table. The Table of Stone is a picture of the Law, presented on stone tablets to Moses. The Law was given as a schoolmaster to show man his need for a Savior. But in the hands of Satan, it is an instrument of destruction. While the White Witch and her dwarf, with Edmund in tow, are approaching their meeting with Aslan, she considers whether or not to kill Edmund. She reflects that the proper place to kill a traitor is the Stone Table.

When the White Witch demands justice, everyone is confounded, for Aslan does not dispute her claims. His followers grope vainly for a solution. The bull puts on a show of force, much as Peter did when he cut off the ear of the high priest's slave. But force cannot overcome the Deep Magic. Susan asks Aslan if he can work something against the Deep Magic, just as Peter tried to deter Christ from the cross. But Aslan's frown silences that request. God's mercy does not contradict His justice. It works with and transcends it.

Ultimately the pact is made. All Aslan's followers know is that Edmund is free, but they don't comprehend the price. Christ's followers, too, knew that Jesus had come to set them free. Not only did the disciples misunderstand what they were to be freed from (they thought the Romans were the problem, rather than sin), but they also were unaware of the terrible price the Messiah would have to pay.

Lewis vividly portrays the sorrow and heaviness that come upon Aslan as death approaches. Matthew's description of Christ says He was deeply grieved to the point of death, and Lewis shows what he meant. When Peter asks Aslan a question, he rouses him from a deep reverie. His voice is dull, he sighs deeply, and his mood dampens everyone's spirits. When Aslan leaves camp for his midnight rendezvous, he is intercepted by Susan and Lucy, who enact a scene comparable to that which took place at Gethsemane. The girls can't sleep and beg to accompany Aslan as far as they can. He, like Christ, is glad to have company, and they support him on the way to his destiny with death. The girls do not say much, but they can at least establish physical contact.

The Narnian story is unlike the biblical account here. Christ's disciples did not give Him the same support.

Their eyes were too heavy to watch and pray with Him in the garden. The spiritual malaise that affected the rest of the world at that darkest of times overshadowed them as well. They could not even be shamed into support. After his brief burst of bravado with his sword, Peter became the greatest coward of the lot. On the other hand, Susan and Lucy's behavior is a heroic reaction of people whose leader is oppressed. Lewis shows just how defeated and drugged by the devil the disciples were during Christ's last days. When Aslan leaves the girls, they cry bitterly, in marked contrast to Peter, who wept for a very different reason.

During Aslan's slaying, many parallels to the crucifixion emerge. Aslan makes no noise when he is bound, a picture of the silent Christ before Pilate and the people. Aslan's mane is shorn as roughly as Christ's cloak was stripped from Him. Instead of a crown of thorns, Aslan is given a muzzle and then kicked, hit, spat upon, and jeered at by the throng. But Aslan's shorn face appears "braver, and more beautiful, and more patient than ever." Likewise, generations of men have seen a stark, unearthly beauty in the mutilated, dying Christ. Instead of a cross, there is the Stone Table; and instead of a spear, a knife. The scene takes place in the darkness of midnight rather than a dark midday.

After Aslan's death, there are more reminders of the Gospels. Susan and Lucy provide the body of their fallen king with the care Joseph of Arimathea gave to Jesus, though the girls have the help of mice to undo the knots.

They show the same quiet despair manifested by Jesus' followers. They wait, and then comes the deeper magic from before the dawn of time.

Aslan's resurrection is awful in the sense that it fills one with awe. Instead of the veil being rent in the temple, there is "a great cracking, deafening noise," as the Stone Table breaks. But the meaning is the same. The Law has been fulfilled; the firstborn from the dead is now alive.

Like the disciples finding the empty tomb, Lucy thinks they have taken the body away. When Lucy and Susan meet Aslan, they are afraid he might be a ghost. As Christ allows the disciples to touch Him and see the nail prints and feel His wounded side, so Aslan lets the girls cover him with kisses. In one short statement, Aslan gives us the meaning of his death, when he says that if the witch could have looked into the darkness before time, she would have known that "when a willing victim who had committed no treachery was killed in a traitor's stead, the Table would crack and Death itself would start working backwards."

Edmund also has a part in the new birth that is coming to Narnia, though he takes the long way around. He begins by traveling the downward path to the witch's castle and receives his reward of stale bread and water. But there is some sign of repentance on Edmund's part, when the witch turns a happy Christmas party into a still life; for the first time, Edmund feels sorry for someone else. Then, when the witch's winter breaks up, he sees what a petty tyrant she is. She is cruel to the reindeer, and her treatment of them only succeeds in gaining a few extra feet. She obviously is powerless to stop the coming of spring. Her response to the threat posed by Aslan is to forbid the dwarf, on pain of death, to mention his name. But best of all is the evidence of new life in Narnia. The sterility of the witch's way of life is finally lost in a chorus of birds and glades of primroses.

When Edmund finally meets Aslan, he is ready. Though Lewis gives no details of their conversation, it is much like a Christian's first meeting with the Master. When Aslan and the witch bargain for his life, Edmund simply looks at Aslan. The witch's words don't matter. He waits with the rest while the arrangements are accomplished. Lewis's own final entrance into the kingdom was as quiet and as personal. One sunny morning Lewis and his brother left by motorcycle for Whipsnade zoo. "When we set out," said Lewis, "I did not believe that Jesus Christ is the Son of God, and when we reached the zoo I did."

Though Lewis does not describe all of the inner workings of the new birth, he gives a beautiful picture of regeneration in the witch's courtyard. Without Christ, man is as dead as the stone animals. Christ needs to take away men's stony hearts and give them hearts of flesh. The life-giving power of Christ is pictured in Aslan breathing on the stone lion; the flame of life licks along and over and under the stone beast.

The new life is even at work in the witch's house. Aslan tells the revitalized animals to search every dark corner of the castle and find lifeless statues. When one is found, Aslan is called for, and the breath of life is imparted.

The Gift of Christmas

One of the traits of Narnia is that in it things are real that are only mythical in our world. There are the creatures drawn from Greek and Roman mythology, the talking animals, and, most strikingly, Father Christmas. He is much like Santa Claus, only better. Lewis says that we think of Santa Claus as being only funny and jolly. But when the children meet Father Christmas, he is "so big, and so glad, and so real" that they are solemn and still, yet glad, in his presence.

In Narnia, there is no competition between Santa Claus and the celebration of Jesus' birth. Father Christmas is subservient to and works for Aslan. His last words to the children are "Long live the true King!" His presence heralds the coming of Christmas, something the witch had always kept from happening.

Father Christmas brings gifts: not just toys, but tools. He gives the children things they will need in their struggle with the witch. In the same way, spiritual gifts of the Holy Spirit are for the Christian's use in the struggle with Satan. Peter's gift of a sword and shield is "the whole armor of God" of the believer (Eph. 6:13). Susan receives a bow, a quiverful of arrows, and a horn that will bring help whenever it is blown. Lucy's gift, a diamond bottle full of cordial that can heal all wounds, suggests the gift of healing.

The gifts are given to be used, and the children have ample opportunity to do so. Peter uses his sword to kill one of the witch's wolves. Susan does not use her gifts in this book, but they play a key role in *Prince Caspian*. Lucy's gift is most important of all in restoring those injured in the battle with the witch, but when the time comes to use it, she has already forgotten about it. Aslan has to remind her of the bottle. Then he must be stern with her to persuade her to leave Edmund and help the animals that have been wounded. Lewis is giving a lesson that spiritual gifts should not be held back. Once a spiritual gift is given, it is not taken away, though it may be misused or ignored. Aslan suggests this when he tells the children, "Once a king or queen in Narnia, always a king or queen."

When the children return to England, the professor repeats this phrase. He tells them that they cannot return to Narnia on their own power, but they have not lost Narnia. The door of the wardrobe will never again lead to Narnia, but when they are needed, Aslan will provide a way for them to return. Their mission has been accomplished for the time; but they will return to Narnia, just as the professor has foretold.

3

The Horse and His Boy

The Horse and His Boy is, more than any of the other Narnia books, a pure adventure story. Like everything that Lewis wrote, it contains intimations of immortality and Christian truth. But these intimations are much less pronounced than they were, for example, in *The Lion, the Witch and the Wardrobe*, where Christ's crucifixion is vividly illuminated, or even *The Silver Chair*, where the philosophical concept of existential reality and the Christian concept that God's light can penetrate even the gates of hell are prominent. Lewis loved a good story, and he proved he could tell one in this engrossing book; in addition, Lewis's baptized imagination teaches some important truths.

It is obvious from the first page that *The Horse and His Boy* is inspired by and draws heavily on the formulas and mood of *The Arabian Nights*. These stories from the Middle East became very popular in England during the eighteenth century and are part of the standard lore to which children are exposed, along with *Grimm's Fairy Tales* and *Mother Goose*. Although Lewis's book does not refer to genies or bottles, the literary atmosphere is strongly reminiscent of the Islamic, fatalistic, and desertic tone of the tales from Arabia. Lewis replaces Allah with Tash and Mecca with Tashbaan, but his impressions of Islam are not disguised by changing the names.

The Tisroc's Realm

The poor fisherman, Arsheesh, exemplifies the hard, grasping nature of life in the land of Calormen. A good mood for him is one when he says nothing to his adopted slave, Shasta. But when his fish sells poorly in the market, he takes out his frustrations by beating Shasta. When he is too lazy to do that, he simply puts off any questions Shasta asks him by engaging in the Calormene national pastime of quoting the poets. And the poets almost always speak in apothegms such as, "Application to business is the root of prosperity, but those who ask questions that do not concern them are steering the ship of folly towards the rock of indigence."

Christians are often accused of having a simplistic approach to life and of quoting the Bible at every opportunity, whether it is relevant or not. But no Christian could do that with the consistency displayed by the Calormenes. They have a quotation for every situation, and there is usually an apothegm for both sides of every issue. The winner in any argument is the one who knows the most poetry. This weakness of the Calormenes may be a lesson to Christians to read the Bible with understanding. It is not enough simply to memorize the words. The Holy Spirit must apply the truth to the believer's heart so that when he speaks, he is speaking in the Spirit, with knowledge. Then the Word will become a two-edged sword, penetrating to the root of the problem, and not a heavy, moralistic club that kills everything it touches.

Lewis describes Arsheesh as having a very practical mind. There is no affection between him and Shasta. The Tarkaan who comes to visit him rightly discerns that Arsheesh is only interested in what he can get out of Shasta. "It is enough to know that you took the child—and have had ten times the worth of his daily bread out of him in labour, as anyone can see." The visit of the Tarkaan also emphasizes the Calormene principle of groveling before everyone who is higher in the social order. Arsheesh and Shasta prostrate themselves before the Tarkaan and offer him all they have, even though they have no love for him. Submission in Calormen is not voluntary.

The real nature of Calormene society comes through when the Tarkaan offers to buy Shasta from Arsheesh. Slavery is common and is no problem for the Calormenes, since the individual has no worth and only has meaning in terms of those he can control. If a man can buy or command no one, he has no meaning. Arsheesh can, of course, control Shasta. But the Tarkaan is offering him a chance to increase his buying power, so a greedy look comes into his face and a wheedling tone comes into his voice. After lying about Shasta's origin and being found out, Arsheesh and the Tarkaan get down to serious negotiation. Shasta hears the whole conversation because he has never been told not to eavesdrop.

This whole passage emphasizes the moral paucity of the Calormenes. Their whole moral system is only as deep as their banal sayings. After everyone grows tired of quoting the poets, he or she simply ends up doing what he or she can get away with. If a Calormene feels bad, he takes it out on those under his feet. He is always respectful to his superiors but is always looking for ways to take advantage of them, too. The ultimate success story in Calormen is the person who manages to claw his way up the pecking order, regardless of what method he uses to get there. The end justifying the means really is a way of life in that southern land.

The spiritual poverty of the Tisroc's realm becomes even clearer when Aravis tells her life story. It is only fair to point out, however, that despite all the negative things brought out in her story, the story itself is a pure delight. Whatever faults the Calormenes are guilty of, they do know how to tell a story. That explains why Lewis was intrigued with *The Arabian Nights*—because the authors of those tales were likewise master storytellers—and why *The Horse and His Boy* became a part of the Narnia books.

But enchanting words cannot hide the fact that even a Tarkheena cannot avoid being treated like a piece of property by her father. The motivation for Arsheesh to sell Shasta to the Tarkaan is monetary gain, and the motivation for Aravis's father to offer her to Ahoshta in marriage is political influence, as well as peace at home. When a greater man orders a lesser man to take action in Calormen, there are only two choices: One is instant obedience, and the other is suicide. Aravis chooses the latter. She is prevented from killing herself by something from outside her world—a talking horse of Narnia.

Aravis is a mixture of positive and negative qualities. She is courageous: After crying for a day about the proposed marriage to Ahoshta, she dries her tears and prepares for the desperate action that she sees as her only way out. She is intelligent: After learning about Narnia, she concocts a brilliant plan for escaping from her father's house, while making him think she is obedient to his wishes. And she is loyal to those who are on her side: When Shasta suspects he may have been left at Tashbaan, Lewis tells us, "She was proud and could be hard enough but she was as true as steel and would never have deserted a companion, whether she liked him or not." But she does not mind exposing her maid to a beating for sleeping late after being drugged. She is contemptuous of Shasta's character and upbringing, and she is aware of her own importance as a Tarkheena. Aravis is, in fact, one of the finest products of Calormene society. It is a sad commentary on that society that it nearly forced her to commit suicide.

The acme of Calormene culture is the city of Tashbaan. It is a distillation of everything important in the land of Calormen. Seen from the top of a ridge, it is magnificent, with its high walls and towers and terraces and gardens and the great temple of Tash and the palace of the Tisroc. The city brings out the worst in Aravis. She becomes even haughtier to Shasta and longs to ride in on a litter attended by slaves, with criers clearing the way before her.

But the splendor of the city dulls on closer acquaintance. The streets are jammed with people who jostle one another without a thought. The common people are always being stopped to make way for an important personage. In the finer streets, great statues of the gods and heroes of Calormen are "mostly impressive rather than agreeable to look at." Pervading all is the stink of Tashbaan, "which came from unwashed people, unwashed dogs, scent, garlic, onions, and the piles of refuse which lay everywhere." In short, the city, which is awesome from the outside, is rotten on the inside.

Lewis's description of Tashbaan parallels John's description of the great whore, Babylon, in Revelation 17:4. John says: "The woman was clothed in purple and scarlet, and adorned with gold and precious stones and pearls, having in her hand a gold cup full of abominations and of the unclean things of her immorality" (NASB). Babylon represents a corrupt world system that, like sin, initially attracts people. But those who drink from that abominable cup find that the dregs are bitter. Likewise, Shasta, Aravis, Bree, and Hwin find that the stink of Tashbaan outweighs the thrill of power one gets from visiting the capital city of a great empire. Tash is the god of power, but he cannot make force beautiful.

The Narnian visitors to the Tisroc's city offer an interesting contrast to the Calormenes. As the Narnians walk the streets, they are considered important enough to have a crier prepare the way in the city where "there is only one traffic regulation, which is that everyone who is less important has to get out of the way for everyone who is more important; unless you want a cut from a whip or a punch from the butt end of a spear." But they do not ride on litters carried by slaves.

> And instead of being grave and mysterious like most Calormenes, they walked with a swing and let their arms and shoulders go free, and chatted and laughed. One was whistling. You could see that they were ready to be friends with anyone who was friendly and didn't give a fig for anyone who wasn't.

Tashbaan also brings out the worst in Shasta. When he is adopted by the Narnians, he pretends, by his silence, to be Corin, who is his look-alike. Living with Arsheesh has taught him never to tell adults anything, if he can avoid it. He even considers abandoning his friends and returning to Narnia by ship as Prince Corin, while leaving the real Corin behind. When the real Corin shows up, Shasta realizes he must leave. But he only advises Corin to tell the truth after it becomes apparent that no lie will be believed. When Shasta tells Corin, "You'll just have to tell them the truth, once I'm safely away," Corin angrily replies, "What else did you think I'd be telling them?" It is obvious that growing up in Archenland encourages truth, while growing up in Calormen encourages lies and deception.

Another indicator of the moral climate of Tashbaan is Aravis's friend Lasaraleen. Lasaraleen is caught up in the social whirl of Tashbaan. She is enthralled with clothes and parties and gossip. She does not share Aravis's interest in sport and animals and the country. Lasaraleen's world is artificial and selfish and silly and largely based on imagination. She retains just enough affection for her friend to help her, but she really cares only about the impression she makes on other people. After spending a day and a half with her, Aravis reaches the startling conclusion that she likes Shasta better than this pampered, empty-headed creature.

The wisdom of the world of Calormen reaches its fullest expression in the scene where the Tisroc and Grand Vizier (Aravis's intended husband) counsel a very rash Prince Rabadash. The scene begins, appropriately, with two deaf and dumb slaves walking backward in front of the Tisroc. The slaves symbolize the condition of Calormen. No one is looking ahead to face the future. Everyone is walking blindly backward, with his eyes focused on those who have control over him. Morally speaking, the followers of the Tisroc are deaf and dumb. They cannot hear the truth, and they cannot speak their minds. The leaders are no better. They are going nowhere in particular, and their eyes are fixed only on the admiring multitudes. Like Lasaraleen, who wants only to be carried through the streets with her new dress on, the leaders want the adulation that comes with power but do not accept the responsibility of protecting those who yield them their allegiance.

Rabadash shows the hypocrisy behind all of the elevated expressions used by the Calormenes. Lewis informs the reader that the prince says, "'Oh-my-father-and-oh-the-delight-of-my-eyes,' . . . very quickly and sulkily and not at all as if the Tisroc *were* the delight of his eyes." This hypocrisy becomes even more plain when he says that the High King Peter of Narnia will want his nephew and grandnephew on the throne of Calormen and, therefore, will not oppose Rabadash's marriage to Susan. This, of course, is contrary to the ridiculous desire, as stated by all Calormenes, for the Tisroc to live forever. Not only does the prince show that he does not believe Calormene truisms, he also demonstrates that he is tired of having the poets quoted to him, by kicking the chief quoter, Ahoshta. Finally, Rabadash seals his own doom by proposing a dash across the desert to Archenland and Narnia.

The Tisroc and Grand Vizier are only too eager to accept Rabadash's proposal, for despicable reasons. Ahoshta wants revenge on the toe that has been kicking him, while the Tisroc wouldn't mind eliminating his son's potential threat to his life. Cowardice keeps the Tisroc from making war on Narnia, but he approves Rabadash's plan for invading it, provided he is not implicated in the action.

The Tisroc approves of the Grand Vizier in a condescending way, because Ahoshta is a clever flatterer and knows all the right quotations. It is humorous to hear him praise Calormene poetry because it is "full of choice apothegms and useful maxims." Aravis correctly assesses his character by calling him "a hideous groveling slave who flatters when he's kicked but treasures it all up and hopes to get his own back by egging on that horrible Tisroc to plot his son's death."

A Free Narnian in Command

The horse in *The Horse and His Boy*, Bree, is a Narnian talking horse who, as a foal, was captured by Calormenes. Like most talking animals, he is superior, both physically and mentally, to ordinary animals of his species. As a result, however, he has a big head. Bree is very much impressed with his valor as a war horse and is not afraid to tell everyone about it. One of the principal themes of the book is the importance of learning humility.

Bree is "a strong dappled horse with flowing mane and tail." When he discovers that his master, the Tarkaan Anradin, is bargaining with Arsheesh for Shasta, he sees his chance to escape to Narnia with Shasta as his rider. He recognizes in Shasta a fellow northerner, and he takes pity on the boy, who would be horribly used by Anradin once the sale was consummated.

So Bree takes charge. He tells Shasta his story, convinces him that they can escape together, cleverly avoids leaving any trail Anradin can follow, and heads north. He is condescending but kind to Shasta. Lewis calls Bree a rude but patient teacher. Over the weeks, he teaches Shasta how to keep his seat under all riding conditions, though, at the end, he tells Shasta he still rides like a sack.

Bree makes all the decisions on this journey and expects Shasta to go along. When Shasta questions whether or not taking the Tarkaan's money is stealing, Bree calls it booty and says they can get no food without it. In other words, it's right because it's necessary. When they steal items such as rope from farms, Bree calls it "raiding." Like many humans, he has a tendency to rationalize questionable behavior when it suits his interests. However, Bree tends to put off the hard decisions, like deciding how they are to get through Tashbaan.

Bree is very conscious of his image. He is anxious to know whether Narnian horses roll and asks that question of Shasta and Hwin. Shasta tells him that the main thing is getting to Narnia. Bree's concern for his appearance is apparent, too, when Hwin suggests shortening their tails for the trip through Tashbaan. Bree is inordinately proud of his tail and objects that it would be very unpleasant to reach Narnia with a ragged tail; but he finally sees the wisdom of Hwin's contention that the objective is arrival, with or without a tail. Bree is like the rich young ruler who came to Jesus. He, too, wanted to do the right thing, but was unwilling to part with something that was very dear to him—his wealth—in order to attain eternal life.

As the journey progresses, Bree's behavior increasingly becomes a problem. He rightly decides to join forces with Hwin and Aravis when he and Shasta involuntarily meet those two travelers. And when Aravis objects to Bree talking to Hwin instead of her, Bree informs her that a talking horse is on the same level as a human. But he does not always assume his role as the leader of the party: Hwin develops the plan for getting through Tashbaan; Shasta discovers how to cross the desert. Bree shows them how to trot and walk their way across the desert, but when they reach the other side, he has his worst lapse.

Bree and Hwin are dog-tired from their trip across the desert, and everyone goes to sleep on the shores of the stream south of Archenland. When he wakes up, Bree insists on being unsaddled and grazing for a while before they head north again. That rest makes the difference between a leisurely stroll into Anvard and a flat-out gallop to the hermit's cabin, pursued by Aslan. Bree has become too easy on himself. Lewis makes the point that "one of the worst results of being a slave and being forced to do things is that when there is no one to force you any more you find you have almost lost the power of forcing yourself." Hwin actually sets the pace, though she is more tired than Bree. When they find themselves hotly pursued by Rabadash, both horses start doing all they think they can do. But it is not until Aslan joins the chase that Bree really puts his ears back and moves.

His motivation, just as it was in Calormen, is fear. That seems to be the only incentive that really stimulates Bree to his best efforts.

Most churches have a few souls like Bree. Some people really take charge and begin well, as Bree does, but peter out in the desert. They lack the stamina and fortitude to follow through on their great plans; they leave that for others. After all, they think, they are willing to think up good ideas in the first place; others should be willing to follow through on them. They want the glory but not the grit.

After the chase is over, Bree starts sulking. His pride has been hurt because Shasta was able to face the menace of the lion, and he was not. He does not enjoy being bested by a peasant boy. Like the Christian who considers a life of sin more exciting than his new life in Christ, he thinks back to his past life of glory in battle. Bree talks foolishly about going back to slavery in Calormen. Some Christians have the same attitude when they feel they have failed God so badly that they cannot be forgiven. Rather than ask forgiveness, they are willing to backslide to their former condition. Fortunately, Bree doesn't really mean to act on his threats, though it sounds like a noble thing to do. The hermit very properly chastises Bree and tells him he is still suffering from conceit. He tells the talking horse that the whole key to his adjustment to life in Narnia is realizing that he is no better than any other Narnian. As long as he continues to compare himself with Calormene horses, he will be unhappy and ridiculous.

Forgetting about his old life in slavery and concentrating on his new life in freedom will turn his attention from himself to others.

Bree is the perfect picture of a reluctant convert, as he heads toward Narnia. Even though he has had his meeting with Aslan, he still wants to wait in Archenland until his tail grows, and he is still concerned whether Narnian horses roll. Lewis says, "He looked more like a horse going to a funeral than a long-lost captive returning to home and freedom."

A few Christians like Bree can easily create the popular impression of Christianity as a negative, joyless religion that takes all the fun out of life. Believers, like Bree, are headed for the Promised Land. If Christians fail to realize the delight that awaits in the presence of God, it is not His fault. Laying aside self-importance is a small price to pay for that joy.

To Narnia and the North

The story of Bree is a progression from a promising beginning to a mediocre ending. Shasta's story is just the opposite. He comes out of unpretentious surroundings, but by the end of the book he has made a good start toward understanding his place in life. His journey from Arsheesh the fisherman's hut through Tashbaan and the desert to Archenland offers parallels with the exodus of the children of Israel from Egypt to the Promised Land.

Shasta's journey, like Lewis's own spiritual pilgrimage, begins in desire. He looks toward the north and longs to know what is beyond the next hill. "One could see nothing but a grassy slope running up to a level ridge and beyond that the sky with perhaps a few birds in it." Similar landscapes also filled the young Lewis with a longing for something he could not put a name to—a longing that was satisfied only by a personal relationship with Christ.

When Shasta asks Arsheesh what lies to the north, he is either cuffed or subjected to poetic maxims. But this response does not cool his ardor. He is thrilled with the news that he is an orphan. It increases his longing to see the world and find his real father. When he tells Bree that he has always longed to go north, Bree tells him it is only natural for him to want to return to the land of his origin.

The same desire for home resides within each human being. Man has come from the hand of God. Though he may be separated from God by sin, there is something within each heart that longs to return home to His presence. This desire takes many forms and is sought for in many places. Some think they will find their heart's desire in a woman or a job or a place or a stimulant or a cause. But all paths lead nowhere, except the ones that lead to God the Father, through Christ and His sacrifice for us. This journey is well documented in Lewis's books *Surprised by Joy* and *The Pilgrim's Regress*. When Shasta and Bree reach the top of the northern ridge that has always intrigued Shasta, it looks "wild and lonely and free." As

Bree observes, what a place for a gallop—straight toward the source of joy!

As their journey continues, the travelers learn more and more about their destination—the land of Narnia. Hwin tells Aravis, for example, that no one in Narnia is forced to marry against her will. The implication is that a commitment to Christ frees one for a truly fulfilling life, because he chooses it—it is not forced upon him. But before the four wanderers can reach Narnia, they must pass through a major obstacle: Tashbaan. The land of Calormen is like the land of Egypt, where the Israelites lived and were captives from the time of Joseph to Moses. Tashbaan and the river that flows around it can be compared with the Red Sea. The Red Sea was a barrier the Israelites could not pass until God made a way through the waters. Tashbaan is a barrier that frustrates the best plan of the two horses and two children.

The land of Egypt was a wonder in its day, full of learning and culture and great buildings. Tashbaan, too, is a wonder in its day. It, like Egypt, is more magnificent than wholesome or refreshing. But it is enough to attract comers from all over the world who would not think of going to the "barbarian" land of Narnia. Egypt had its attractions for the Israelites. Their desire for leeks and onions and garlics in the wilderness seems laughable, but the world of that day exerted just as strong a pull as the world today does.

Ultimately, however, the travelers must strip themselves of all pretensions and emulate the commonest slaves in order to hope to pass through the city. Similarly, the Israelites needed to put their ties with Egypt behind them when they headed for the Promised Land.

The Israelites were given a pillar of cloud by day and a pillar of fire by night to lead them through the wilderness. Shasta is given directions for finding his way through the desert; his pillar of cloud is the double peak of Mount Pire. It is his duty to keep the rest of the party headed toward that objective, even when doing so hurts his eyes and makes his head ache. The fact that he does so without complaining indicates that he is becoming less and less Arsheesh the fisherman's son and more and more Prince Cor of Archenland.

But before he gathers his party at the Tombs of the Ancient Kings and sets out across the desert, Shasta faces one other test: the test of patience. He waits for a night and a day before the two horses and Aravis arrive. Their arrival forestalls his execution of a disastrous plan to set out across the desert by himself. Moses, too, must have grown tired of waiting for his people—especially when he learned they were doomed to spend forty years in the wilderness. The fact that he did wait and wander with the rest made it possible for their children to enter into the new land. And Moses, like Shasta, needed the help of the others to reach and possess the Promised Land.

The journey across the desert north of Calormen is long and hot and weary, especially for the horses, but there is a refreshing pool at the end of their ride. This pool is reminiscent of the well the Lord provided for the Israelites at Beer, where they sang for joy. The only problem is that Aravis, Bree, Shasta, and Hwin make too much of a good thing by going to sleep. They have mistaken a rest stop for the end of the journey. Jesus wants believers to sit down, refresh themselves, and then proceed with His business. If they linger too long, they may turn a spiritual asset into a liability.

The progress that Shasta has been making becomes apparent during the final gallop into Archenland with a lion at their heels. Shasta looks back, sees that Hwin and Aravis are in trouble, jumps off Bree, runs back to the lion, and simply yells at him to go home. Lewis tells us, "He had never done anything like this in his life before and hardly knew why he was doing it now." People who stay in God's will find themselves doing incredible things. The results of their actions are liable to be incredible, too. Shasta's idiotic approach works, and the lion rushes away.

Even then, he learns he is not through. He finds that he must run on foot to find King Lune and warn him of impending danger. He rebels at this momentarily, for he feels his strength is gone. Lewis describes his situation in words that could stand as the motto for this book: "He had not yet learned that if you do one good deed your reward usually is to be set to do another and harder and better one." Shasta must follow his mission through to the end. The path is not the easy one, but it is the road to fulfillment.

Like Shasta, every believer begins his life in the fisherman's hut. Man is spiritually poverty stricken, with a hard taskmaster, Satan, giving him cuffs and menial tasks to perform. God can lead mankind out of the land of bondage, through the sea of sin, over the desert of dryness, into the Promised Land of milk and honey, but only when each man is willing to put himself at God's disposal. "If we have died with him, we shall also live with him; if we endure, we shall also reign with him; if we deny him, he also will deny us; if we are faithless, he remains faithful—for he cannot deny himself" (2 Tim. 2:11–13).

The Lion's Claws

Aslan, as Shasta remarks to Aravis when he tells how he came to live in Calormen, is at the back of all the Narnia stories, including this one. But he assumes a somewhat fiercer character in this book than in the other tales. He roars at and chases the two horses with their riders and scratches Aravis painfully. Actually, he appears in a variety of modes, all of which are consistent with the personality Lewis has been developing in the first four books.

Aslan's first fierce encounter with the four travelers takes place along the Calormene coast. He roars from both sides so that the two horses draw close together and pursues them to the water's edge. When Hwin makes a slip and talks to Aravis, Bree overhears her and encourages Hwin to join with them. The two pairs would have avoided each other like the plague without the fear induced by Aslan's pursuit.

Sometimes a person's first contact with the Lord must be on the basis of fear. He may be too self-satisfied to care about God's claims on his life. So He must allow some frightening experience to throw him off stride and make him see the need for divine intervention. This is not God's preferred method of operation. He would prefer simply to offer repentance, followed by salvation, but it usually isn't that easy. Lewis felt that he was harried into the kingdom. He claimed to be the most reluctant convert in all of England. He accepted God of his own free will, but it was not a will that had sought out the Lord. It was a will that had been backed into a corner and finally had to either admit that God was God or deny everything else.

The next encounter involves Shasta beside the Tombs of the Ancient Kings. He is all alone in the desert that night and is badly in need of some companionship. That need is filled by a large cat. It is not surprising that Aslan should come as a cat in this instance, because Shasta is in need of comforting, not frightening. In the other books Lewis says Aslan appears to be smaller to those who don't know him very well. He grows on better acquaintance and becomes huge when one knows him intimately. The believer's apprehension of the Lord grows, too, as he spends time with Him. He may seem small and powerless against the powerful forces of evil when one first meets Him. But eventually the Christian realizes that He really does have the whole world in His hands.

The cat leads Shasta through the tombs to the desert side and then offers him a warm backstop against the desert, while Shasta lies down with his face toward the tombs. When jackals begin to close in during the night, Aslan becomes a lion again and roars them away. This relieves Shasta, and he tells Aslan how grateful he is. He also says he will never be mean to a cat again, as he once was. Aslan scratches him, presumably because Shasta needs to know how it feels to be victimized. Aravis receives the same lesson later, but her punishment is much more severe, because her deed was more damaging. Shasta tries to make the cat talk, but the cat just stares at him. Perhaps Shasta needs to become better acquainted with Aslan before verbal communication is desirable or possible.

Aravis's punishment takes place in a terrible scene in which Aslan rushes headlong at Aravis and Hwin; he causes Hwin to let out a bloodcurdling horse scream and leaves Aravis with ten scratches. This is the most difficult episode in the book to understand, because it seems so out of character for a loving and merciful creator. But Lewis explains in *The Lion, the Witch and the Wardrobe* that Aslan is not a tame lion. He has roared several times. He tells Jill in *The Silver Chair* that he has swallowed whole realms, and he will do that in *The Last Battle*. But his attack on Aravis looks more devastating than it really is. One reason for it is that it causes the horses to reach the hermit in time. Also, Aravis's wounds match, stroke for stroke, those given her maid, whom she had drugged. But why isn't Aslan merciful and forgiving in this instance?

The reason is that Aravis does not think she needs mercy. She is very cool about the incident and, in general, is implacable toward her enemies. The strokes give her the wisdom caused by pain.

After being wounded, Aravis is a different person: She does not feel bitter or defeated; she even feels fortunate not to have been cut more deeply. The Christian parallel may be found in Isaiah 53:5: "With his stripes we are healed." Sometimes, however, the believer is not ready to accept God's provision. So he must receive some of the stripes himself. There is a saying that either a man accepts the atonement or he repeats it. Aravis repeats it until she is ready to apologize so that she can stay in Archenland.

Shasta learns some lessons from Aslan, too. He is feeling sorry for himself, since he seems to have all the work to do and ends up in the cold. While Bree and Aravis and Hwin are with the hermit, Shasta is left to wander blindly along an unmarked road. When Aslan joins him in the fog, Shasta does not know who he is, but he can tell he is a large creature. When he tells his story to Aslan, the lion does not agree with Shasta that he is unfortunate.

When Shasta realizes who the lion is, a holy fear replaces his terror. When he sees the lion, he is huge; Shasta now knows enough of the lion to see him in his true form. The boy is awestruck with Aslan's beauty and loses the feeling that he has been persecuted and misused. When Aslan vanishes, he leaves behind a fountain of life, springing up from his footstep, which refreshes Shasta.

The analogy to the living water of Jesus is unmistakable. Shasta learns later that Aslan has walked between him and disaster on the edge of a cliff. It was necessary for him to take this dangerous route in order to warn the Narnians of the presence of Rabadash at Anvard. Shasta is not through with danger. He rides into battle with the Narnians, totally unprepared to defend himself. But he now has a sense of direction for his actions, through Aslan's guidance, and he later discovers a new identity as Prince Cor of Archenland.

Meanwhile, Bree is making a fool out of himself by claiming that Aslan is not a lion. He cannot see how Aslan could be one of the creatures who frighten him so badly. So he babbles on blithely about how ridiculous it is to believe that Aslan could have four paws and a tail and whiskers, when suddenly he is tickled by one of Aslan's whiskers. Bree is like those liberal theologians who rail against anthropomorphism and claim that God could not have assumed human form. Bree is cured of his Calormen-bred stupidity by a whisker in his ear.

The last character who needs to feel the lion's claws is Rabadash. Rabadash the Rash has made himself Rabadash the Ridiculous by catching himself neatly on a hook in the midst of battle. He pleads for an opponent to engage in armed combat, but he is refused that privilege by King Lune, since he has not acted honorably in attacking Anvard. King Lune does his best to make Rabadash listen to reason, but the Tisroc's heir flies off in volatile bursts of invective against Narnia and Archenland and Aslan and Queen Susan. Even Aslan cannot bring him to his senses. So Aslan applies the only real cure for Rabadash's self-importance: He makes him look as ridiculous as he is. Becoming a donkey is something his pride can't take, but he brings that punishment on himself. Aslan ensures that all of the Calormenes know what Rabadash has been before he is changed back to his human form. The result is that Rabadash becomes a very peaceable Tisroc, not through virtue but through fear of becoming a donkey again. Once again fear plays a legitimate role in bringing out the best in people.

Lewis offers a clear choice in this book. Man can either take the easy way of recognizing his inadequacy and turning to the Lord's provision and mercy, or he can risk incurring the wrath of God, which is often motivated as much by a desire for man's salvation as by a determination to see justice done. God can come either way—as a lion or as a lamb. If a man rejects the Lamb of God who takes away the sins of the world, he must expect the Lion of Judah to avenge the insult of this rejection of His Father's provision.

4

Prince Caspian

The Lion, the Witch and the Wardrobe represents the Golden Age of Narnia. In Lewis's grand chronology of Narnian history, *Prince Caspian* moves on to the Narnian Middle Ages. The golden days of kings Peter and Edmund and queens Susan and Lucy have, through many intervening years, given way to the onslaught of the Telmarine barbarians. The Telmarines have not only taken possession of the land, they have also done their utmost to obliterate the native Narnians: the talking animals, centaurs, fauns, satyrs, and other creatures which are thought of as mythological.

The new rulers of Narnia are barbaric in other ways, too. They care for nothing but the martial arts—those skills that will help them subdue and dominate their enemies and subjects. Studies that do not aid in achieving these ends are not worthy of their consideration. Caspian's uncle, Miraz, is particularly incensed to hear that

Caspian has been listening to "silly stories" about Old Narnia—the period in Narnian history when the talking animals were its principal occupants. The ignorance of the Telmarines can also be seen in their unreasoning fear of anything they do not understand, such as navigation and bodies of water. They do not believe in Aslan, but they know that all the old stories say he comes from over the sea, so they superstitiously let the woods grow up between themselves and the sea.

Medieval Narnia

Lewis was well qualified to write a book based on the Middle Ages, because he knew as much as anyone about the intellectual and imaginative crosscurrents that shaped the medieval mind. Years before he became professor of medieval and renaissance literature at Cambridge University, Lewis wrote *Allegory of Love*, a literary criticism that explores the development of the chivalric romance, with its woman-deifying conception of love. This landmark in its field made Lewis's reputation as a scholar.

Lewis sets the medieval mood by dropping the Pevensie children into a ruined castle. Lewis was fascinated by such places. He loved to wander through them and dream of the days when they were filled with shouts and songs and laughter. The noises have died away, and there is a feeling of peaceful repose. He catches this mood by describing the ruins of Cair Paravel as "a bright, secret, quiet place, and rather sad." Its perimeter is choked with vegetation, but inside there are grass and daisies covered only by the sky. It is almost as if the restless world has beaten its way right to the door but cannot get in to disturb the calm. Lewis once wrote a description of Tintern Abbey, which sounds very much like Cair Paravel:

> It is an abbey practically intact except that the roof is gone, and the glass out of the windows, and the floor, instead of a pavement, is a trim green lawn. Anything like the *sweetness* and peace of the long shafts of sunlight falling through the windows on the grass cannot be imagined. All churches should be roofless. A holier place I never saw.

Lewis builds on the medieval mood of this book by showing the typical curriculum of a young prince during the period. Caspian studies cosmography (geography), rhetoric (speech), heraldry (the study of family trees and coats of arms), versification (poetry), history, law, physic (medicine), alchemy (turning base metals to gold), and astronomy. Typical of his textbooks is the *Grammatical Garden or the Arbour of Accidence pleasantlie open'd to Tender Wits*, by Pulverulentus Siccus. In today's terminology, this might be translated as *An Elementary Grammar for Young Minds*, by Dry Dust. Caspian also learns to play the recorder and the theorbo. The recorder is a flutelike instrument, and the theorbo was a stringed instrument similar to a lute or guitar. Finally, Caspian learns all of those manly and warlike skills so important to his uncle

Miraz. These include sword fighting, riding, bowman-ship, and hunting.

Two of the more controversial parts of Caspian's education are astronomy and magic. His tutor, Doctor Cornelius, is a minor magician; and Caspian is taught to believe that the conjunction of two planets, Tarva and Alambil, means that some great good will come to Narnia. Their meeting is described as a dance involving the Lord of Victory and the Lady of Peace. This is possible in Narnia, where the stars have personalities.

Many people in the Middle Ages believed in white magic and black magic. Black magic was practiced by corrupt individuals for self-seeking or perverted reasons. A few people were reputed to manipulate forces for good ends. The character of Merlin in the tales of King Arthur is a good example. Without exactly buying this theory, Lewis believed that many gray areas that used to be nei-ther good nor bad in themselves are becoming clearer and clearer with the passage of time. The whole universe is gradually coming into focus. The only supernatural forces now operating are God and the devil. Either we are empowered by the Lord or we are being led astray by Satan, or we are in a more or less powerless state in between. Doctor Cornelius's magic should be accepted as a standard element in a fairy tale. He does nothing very significant with his powers, beyond putting some of the servants to sleep and locating Caspian's party.

Lewis obviously enjoyed filling in all the details to create a medieval mood. Some parts of the picture don't seem typical of the Middle Ages. The towns and civilization of Telmarine Narnia seem more modern than that. However, by the thirteenth and fourteenth centuries, the feudal system of land ownership was breaking down in England, towns were springing up and growing, and trade guilds were becoming prominent. Medieval politics are faithfully portrayed as well: The sudden shifts of fortune occurring because of the birth of an heir, a relative of the king killing him to gain his kingdom, and the usurper's friends deserting him to gain a larger share of the action were all characteristic of the era of kings. Lucy correctly observes, "It's worse than the Wars of the Roses."

Even in the smallest details, Lewis is faithful to his model. When a coin is tossed to see whether Trumpkin or Susan will shoot first at the apple, Trumpkin is interested because he has never before observed a coin toss to decide an issue. The coin toss is a relatively modern invention, and doubtful questions back to Jesus' time and before were usually decided by casting lots. But all this attention to detail provides only the setting for this book. Lewis tells a story in which a number of cardinal truths are depicted.

Soulish Beasts

Prince Caspian is about talking animals. They are the true inhabitants of Narnia (the Old Narnians); Narnia was made for them. When he was a small boy, Caspian hears stories from his nurse and longs to meet them. Most of the other Telmarines hate and fear talking animals, and they especially fear Aslan. A talking animal, Trufflehunter the Badger, is the first to befriend Caspian in his adversity, and talking animals are the bulk of Caspian's army. They are the main characters in the book.

The talking animals in *Prince Caspian* illustrate the meaning of the soul. It is easy to say that men possess souls and animals do not, but saying that can have a hazy meaning. When one puts souls into animals, as Lewis does, the meaning of the soul becomes clear. After Trufflehunter befriends Caspian, Nikabrik accuses Caspian of hunting beasts for sport. Caspian admits that he has, but that he hasn't killed any talking animals. Nikabrik claims that killing one is as bad as killing the other, but he is quickly corrected by Trufflehunter. Hunting dumb animals is done for sport or based on the necessity for food; hunting talking animals is murder.

Trufflehunter shows that the external appearance of a man or an animal is not the really significant thing; the essential characteristic is whether or not a creature possesses reason, the ability to talk, and a spiritual dimension. The spiritual dimension, in this case, is the awareness that Aslan is the king of beasts and that one attains true fulfillment in his service. At first Caspian is stunned by the fact that the long-nosed face that is talking about him belongs to a badger. But he soon learns that Trufflehunter is much more friendly to him and more right-minded than the more manlike dwarf, Nikabrik.

Each talking animal possesses a soul, as men do, but the animals are not disguised people. Each has its own peculiar beastly characteristics. Trufflehunter is always proud to claim that he is a beast, and beasts don't change, unlike the forgetful dwarfs. As a badger, he holds on. Even though Aslan has not been in Narnia for centuries, Trufflehunter remembers all the old stories about Aslan and has no doubt of his existence. He also remembers that Narnia was never right unless a son of Adam was king. This was a hard truth to retain in a land where humans were trying to destroy anything wild. Finally, Trufflehunter never forgets that he is a badger and never pretends he is a human or a dwarf. When he is offered armor for the impending battle, he prefers to rely on his own teeth and claws for protection.

Trufflehunter is faithful when the darkest hour comes to Caspian's army in the Mound of the Stone Table late one night. With Peter, Edmund, and Trumpkin waiting in the passage, Trufflehunter states that Aslan will send help and that it may even then be at the door. After weary days of battle and the seeming failure of Susan's horn, this is a hard thing to say. But his statement is literally true. God really is in the wings, waiting to send needed help just when circumstances are the ugliest. Trufflehunter is justly rewarded with a kiss from the High King Peter.

The other beasts also behave according to their species. Caspian encounters the three Bulgy Bears in an apparent state of hibernation. When they sleepily recognize him as their king, Caspian is feasted on sticky honey without bread. At Dancing Lawn, the Bulgies are much more interested in feasting than in holding a council of war. And, though they insist on providing a marshal of the lists for Peter's combat with Miraz, the selected bear cannot help sucking his paws and looking uncommonly silly.

Pattertwig the squirrel is an incessant chatterer, is eager to carry messages through the trees, feasts Caspian with a nut (after Caspian is warned not to look while he fetches it), and volunteers to travel to western Narnia in case the High Kings and Queens should be there. At Dancing Lawn, he is so excited and eager to please that it is nearly impossible to get him to stop yelling "Silence!"

But the real charmer in *Prince Caspian* and *The Voyage of the* Dawn Treader is Reepicheep. He is a merry and martial mouse with a tiny rapier at his side and a habit of twirling his whiskers like a mustache. He is absolutely without fear and has a keen sense of his own honor. The biggest fool in Narnia, the Giant Wimbleweather, is an object of derision to him. Reepicheep has a band of eleven followers who, as Caspian observes, could easily be put in a wash basket. The mouse is disappointed when he is not chosen to deliver the challenge to Miraz and when he is not selected as a marshal of the lists. Only Peter's diplomatic assurances that a mouse might frighten the enemy manage to pacify him.

Reepicheep gets his chance to be brave and useful in the last battle with Miraz's army. While all the others are fighting four or five feet in the air, Reepicheep and his followers are at ground level, sticking pins in the Telmarines' legs. Reepicheep is more zealous than all the rest and receives the most serious wounds. He is practically a corpse when his followers carry him, on a litter, to Aslan. Lucy takes care of his wounds with cordial from her little diamond bottle, but his tail is missing. Reepicheep is lost without his tail, since it is "the honour and glory of a Mouse." When Aslan gently reminds him that he is perhaps a bit too concerned about his honor, Reepicheep responds that creatures as small as mice need to take great pains to guard their dignity. Aslan is not convinced, but he yields when all the other mice prepare to cut off their own tails if their leader is not permitted to have one. Because of the love the mice have for their leader and because the mice were responsible for chewing away the cords that bound Aslan to the Stone Table many years before, Aslan gives Reepicheep a tail.

Reepicheep *is* a little too concerned about his personal dignity, and his attempts to defend it against anyone, including Giant Wimbleweather, really are a little ridiculous. But despite his touchiness on this subject, Reepicheep thrives on real opposition. Overwhelming odds do not bother him. The fight with Miraz is his chance to prove he meant all those brave words, and it offers an outlet for his irrepressible courage.

Lewis gives a chilling reminder of man's destiny if his heritage as a soulish creature is forgotten. When the children are attacked by a wild bear in the woods, Susan delays shooting it because it may be a talking beast. Trumpkin informs her that "most of the beasts have gone enemy and gone dumb, but there are still some of the other kind left." Christians living in the flesh will develop weak, ineffectual souls that have "gone dumb."

In the Lion's Tracks

The heart of *Prince Caspian* is the journey of Peter, Susan, Edmund, Lucy, and Trumpkin from Cair Paravel to the hill of the Stone Table. *The Lion, the Witch and the Wardrobe* contains a journey into sin; *Prince Caspian* is a journey into discipleship. The story deals with the development of four disciples and one skeptic.

In New Testament terms, Peter fills the role of the leader, the apostle Paul. Edmund is the wiser, postascension Peter. Lucy is the loving disciple, John. Susan becomes increasingly like Judas. Although this may seem harsh, since she does follow the others and apologize to Lucy, she eventually shows her true colors in unmistakable terms.

The journey begins in Cair Paravel. The ruined castle represents the children's return to a thrilling, rather distant, and somewhat hazy past experience. At first they don't recognize their castle, but they begin to piece the puzzle together, and the old days revive in their memories. The twang of Susan's bowstring brings back memories of battles and hunts and feasts. Even the air starts working on them, and they become more like kings and queens and less like children.

The first hours in Narnia represent some important principles for spiritual growth. When the children return to Narnia, their experience is much like the Christian who looks back on his or her first phase of Christian life. He or she seems to have rediscovered a golden age when the first love of Christ was new and beautiful, events were exciting, and people were a challenge. When the Christian life seems hard, something seen or heard may bring back the joy of those first days in God's family. Even a sound, like the twang of a bowstring, may result in exhilarating stabs of pleasure.

The children are rediscovering their first meeting with Aslan as they return to Cair Paravel. When they left Narnia at the end of the Golden Age, they were maturing into real kings and queens. But when they returned to this world, they became children again. Living in Narnia represents living in the Spirit, and living in this world represents living in the flesh, because the children have not yet discovered the earthly equivalent of Aslan. Living after the desires of the flesh results in loss of spiritual maturity.

After the Pevensies discover that the ruined castle is Cair Paravel, they look for their old treasure chamber. When they find it, the most precious treasures are the gifts from Father Christmas. It is as if their spiritual gifts were put away in a chamber for safekeeping. They have not been destroyed by time: Peter's sword is not rusty, nor is Susan's bowstring perished.

Just remembering the spiritual highlights of the past is not enough. Once the children discover Cair Paravel, recover the gifts, and get some rest, they are ready to move on. They feel that they have to get off that island. Like the New Testament Hebrew believers, they need to be ready to press on to maturity. The apples of Cair Paravel get old after a while, and the children are ready for a more complete diet. They love Cair Paravel and the past's memories, but they know the castle is only the starting point for their journey. They have a mission to perform, and they are eager to get started.

The little party decides to make the first part of the excursion over water. They have chosen wisely, because the Telmarines are afraid of both water and the woods. At first all goes well. They have made a rational decision, and logic carries them on the right path—right to the canyon of the Rush. At this point, Peter and Edmund become confused. They do not realize the stream is the Rush until Trumpkin logically demonstrates how, through the work of intervening centuries, a gentle river valley could become a wide chasm.

That is as far as logic can take them, but the children do not yet know it. Logic, followed to its bitter end, will lead them into the arrows of the Telmarines. Aslan does not mean them to fly, but the right way for their journey to follow is the seemingly impossible one of scaling the steep cliffs on both sides of the Rush. Aslan will lead them through the valley of the shadow of death, but they must follow him. If they do not follow the seemingly irrational path he sets, their earlier good sense will be for naught. They will fail within sight of their goal, but that will only make their failure more bitter.

In this scene, Lewis is describing the limitations of rational thought. Logic can only take man so far, and then he must rely on faith. Lewis was a brilliant intellectual, but he was also a man of strong faith. Development of the mind is a useful tool, but without the Spirit's guidance, it is useless. The discernment of a need to turn to faith when rational thought reaches an impasse is essential in the Christian life. The Bible is not anti-intellectual, but it sometimes takes a different tack from man. Intellectualism for its own sake can lead to the attitude Lewis despised: a lack of concern for human life and an excessive interest in progress.

The conversation the children and the dwarf have on the edge of the cliff shows the character of each disciple. Peter is initially perplexed by the changes in the Rush since the Golden Age. Even after Trumpkin explains what has happened, he has difficulty coping with his role as the leader. He must cast the deciding vote concerning their direction. Peter doesn't even want to vote, but Trumpkin reminds him of his responsibility as High King. His decision is a cop-out; he decides to go down because "we must do one or the other." Peter reminds one of a defeated Elijah more than the triumphant Paul singing in the Philippian jail.

Susan behaves horribly in this situation. Even before the crucial scene at the Rush, Lewis gives the reader warnings about Susan. When all the others are eager to look for the old treasure chamber, practical Susan complains about how late in the day it is and how drafty and damp a big hole at their backs will be. She does not share the spirit of adventure that has gripped the others. Practicality is both Susan's greatest asset and her biggest liability. Where practicality is needed, she can be invaluable. But where imagination or creativity or faith is needed, she cannot cope.

Susan cannot stand competition, fighting, and death. Lewis informs the reader that she dislikes fighting during the broadsword duel between Edmund and Trumpkin. The children are almost mauled by a wild bear because Susan hates killing things and is slow in discharging her arrow. Her attitude toward competition is clear when she reluctantly beats Trumpkin in an apple-shooting contest. What she fails to appreciate is the fact that the purpose of the competitions is to enlist the support of the skeptical dwarf, who has heard of the old kings and queens, but sees nothing very impressive about the Pevensies. There is always a danger of becoming sinfully proud in competing, but it is also possible for them to compete for the glory and honor of Aslan. Lucy gives the best pattern for action when she is eager to see Trumpkin's shoulder. She does not think of herself as a healer, which could make her proud, but only as a person who has a gift that can meet the need of another.

On the brink of the Rush valley, Susan tries to take the easy way out. She complains that she knew all along they were going wrong. When Lucy tells the others she has seen Aslan, Susan asks her where she *thinks* she saw him. Her technique is like that of Satan in the Garden of

Eden. Satan questions whether or not God really told Eve to eat of every tree save one, and Susan questions whether or not Lucy really saw Aslan. When it is her turn to vote, Susan follows her sense of practicality, which tells her to go out of the woods rather than wander around lost. She is like Judas, the practical member of the twelve. This is shown, in Judas, by the fact that he kept the purse. When we accuse him of being a liar, a cheat, and a traitor from birth, we may be doing him an injustice. At the beginning he was probably attracted to Christ, the same way the others were. When he saw Jesus' effect on the crowds, he may have begun to see the financial wisdom of backing Him; he may have kept the purse to protect his investment. When Judas saw Jesus attacking the hypocrites and envisioned his profits draining away, despair must have gripped him. Not understanding the purpose of Christ's mission, he settled for what he could get: thirty pieces of silver.

Edmund has learned a lot since the first book. Then he was like the cowardly preresurrection Peter. Now he atones for his previous bad behavior toward Lucy; he knows she was right before and is likely to be right again. He has the power of the apostle Peter in the book of Acts.

Lucy has the most difficult role: She is the visionary, the only one who can see Aslan, and the one who must persuade the others to follow an invisible lion. It doesn't seem fair that Lucy should be chosen. She is the youngest and doesn't have a take-charge personality. She is usually willing to go along with the others. It is much more difficult for her to enlist the support of others than it would be for Peter to do it.

Yet it is also logical that Lucy should see Aslan when the others cannot. She is the beloved disciple, the apostle John. She loves Aslan the most, and love has the greatest power to reveal the object of one's desires to him or her. When she sees Aslan, he appears larger to her, because she and her love for Aslan have grown. Lucy is chosen for this job because she is the least-prominent member of the group, and she is the greatest servant.

Being chosen to receive the vision is not unadulterated joy. Lucy is overjoyed to see him and recognizes instantly that they are to follow him, but she encounters immediate skepticism from the others. Susan questions the truth of her vision. Trumpkin says he must be pretty elderly by this time, and he must have turned wild and witless, like other animals. Even Peter, though he is kind to his favorite sister, does not know whether or not to believe her. When the decision is made to head down the Rush, Lucy sees nothing for it but to follow the others, weeping bitterly. Her feelings are those of self-righteous indignation and frustration.

The path out of the woods is hard, exhausting, and leads them into trouble. They must go far out of their way to avoid some young fir woods at the edge of the cliff. When they get down into the valley, they must risk a dangerous climb over slippery rocks with the stream far below them. And just when things start looking better, they run into enemy arrows. Then Lucy suggests, in the mildest way possible, that they take Aslan's route. They must make their way back over the same difficult terrain that caused them so much grief. Attempting to take shortcuts in the Christian life may lead to a similar failure.

In the dead of the night there is a curious reenactment of the previous day's scene by the Rush canyon. Lucy once again sees Aslan; she is overjoyed to be reunited with the one she loves. But this time Aslan must correct her. She has been a faithful witness to her vision of the lion, but she did not forsake the others to follow him. For the first time, she is learning that others must never be put before God. When he has charged her with spiritual vitality, Aslan sends her back to the others, with a more difficult task than before. Not only must they follow an invisible lion; they must also charge up and down cliffs in the middle of the night, after being roused from a deep sleep.

When Lucy tells her story, Trumpkin is still skeptical, and Susan is still hateful. Susan is in the grip of her fears and behaves like a perfect little beast. Even when the others agree to follow Lucy, Susan threatens a sit-down strike. Edmund, however, is still supportive of Lucy, and Peter is too wise to make the same mistake twice.

At first Lucy feels very bitter about Susan's attitude, but she fixes her eyes on Aslan, and her negative emotions disappear. She is too busy watching and following Aslan to worry abut Susan's attitude. This is the attitude of the Christian who is following Christ closely.

Lucy's hot pursuit of Aslan gets her over the edge of the cliff. If she had stopped to think about it, she probably would have balked at the edge. Her faith in Aslan is the basis of her courage.

When they have been following Lucy awhile, the others begin to see Aslan. Edmund sees him first, which is appropriate, since he is the only one who has supported her throughout. Then Peter begins to see him. Peter has been weak and indecisive, but he has not been malicious to Lucy. At last, Susan and Trumpkin see Aslan. Susan is corrected for yielding to her fears and apologizes to Lucy.

The Faithful Skeptic

Trumpkin is the faithful skeptic of *Prince Caspian*. He is the loyal, aggravating, inspiring, bullheaded, rational, ignorant, and moral soul who ties the book together. He is the unifying force that bridges the gap between the spiritual journey of the Pevensies from Cair Paravel to the Stone Table and the struggle of Narnia to free itself from the tyrannical Miraz. Trumpkin is obviously a great favorite of Lewis's.

Trumpkin is modeled after Lewis's tutor of his teenage years. Mr. Kirkpatrick, or "The Great Knock," taught Lewis how to think. Kirkpatrick was an atheist who was quick to correct, could be severe, and was absolutely merciless in exposing sloppy thinking. He was always challenging Lewis to examine his statements and the assumptions behind them. "The Great Knock" could hardly have been an easy man to get along with, but Lewis revered him as his intellectual father. He taught Lewis to be one of the great debaters of his generation. Several of Lewis's biographers have noted that it was impossible to disagree with him. No matter who was right, Lewis could always muster three arguments to every one produced by his opponent.

Lewis's love for this strange man stayed with him throughout his life, and he appears in several forms in Lewis's fiction. The basis of these characters is a very moral man who is committed to following his ideals, but who has somehow missed the basic fact of God's existence. This characteristic of Trumpkin's appears repeatedly in *Prince Caspian*.

Trumpkin has as much cause as anyone to hate and fear the Telmarines, yet he refuses to listen to Nikabrik's suggestion to kill Caspian. Trumpkin perceives that killing the defenseless prince would be an act of murder, and he will have nothing to do with it. When the black dwarf suggests enlisting the aid of some ogres and hags, Trumpkin is again adamant. He does not care that Aslan would not like their presence in camp; all he knows is that they do not square with his moral code.

Trumpkin is continually skeptical. He doubts the Telmarine ghost stories and rightly suspects that the ghosts receive a little assistance from the Telmarine soldiers. He doesn't believe in Aslan or in the stories of the ancient

High Kings and Queens. When Trufflehunter talks about waking the trees and waters, Trumpkin jokes about getting the stones to throw themselves at Miraz. He doesn't believe in the reputed properties of Queen Susan's horn either. He tells Caspian, "I think the Horn—and that bit of broken stone over there—and your great King Peter—and your Lion Aslan—are all eggs in moonshine." But his true character shows through when Nikabrik refuses to leave because the dwarfs might be mistreated. Trumpkin volunteers to journey to Cair Paravel, looking for help, even though he believes no help will come. He says that there is a difference between giving advice and taking orders. He has given his advice and is now willing to take his orders.

When Trumpkin is rescued by the Pevensies, he receives a lesson in what children out of the past can do. But it is not until his hand has been stung by Edmund, he has been outshot by Susan, and he has been healed by Lucy's ointment that Trumpkin is fully ready to believe that the old stories of a Golden Age in Narnia are true. Even then, the dwarf is not ready to believe in Aslan. He babbles about Aslan growing old and witless, until Lucy is ready to fly at him. But his muddled mind does not keep him from following the High King Peter, even in pursuit of an invisible lion. And it is Trumpkin who gets Susan moving when she threatens to stay behind.

Nothing comes easily to Trumpkin, especially faith. When he meets Aslan, the lion shakes the nonsense out of the dwarf just like a man might shake salt out of a shaker.

It is almost inevitable that Trumpkin should meet and believe in Aslan, because, though he was blind to it, he has been on Aslan's side all along.

The Crooked Path to Nowhere

Nikabrik is a perfect foil to Trumpkin. Trumpkin is a red dwarf; Nikabrik is a black dwarf. Trumpkin smokes a pipe; Nikabrik does not smoke. Nikabrik is full of angry thoughts and sour words, while Trumpkin always seems cheerful in his skepticism. The differences in the dwarfs are more than superficial. The two are moral opposites. Trumpkin is deeply committed to a strong moral code, while Nikabrik is for practically nothing but the dwarfs and himself. Trumpkin follows a skeptical, moral path that finally leads him into the presence of Aslan, while Nikabrik's hatred takes him down the crooked path to nowhere.

The difference between the dwarfs comes through in Caspian's first encounter with them. Nikabrik wants to kill Caspian because he is a Telmarine and a human, and the Telmarines have mercilessly persecuted dwarfs. He is enraged to discover that Caspian is the nephew of the Telmarine ruler, and only force can subdue Nikabrik from murdering Caspian on the spot. Hatred burns like a bright flame inside Nikabrik. Trumpkin, on the other hand, adopts a cautious wait-and-see attitude. His moral code tells him he cannot murder a sick, defenseless victim. So he good-humoredly makes the best of the situation.

The black dwarfs finally accept Caspian and Aslan because they are against Miraz. Hatred can be selective, and Nikabrik's hatred of the cruel Miraz is strongest of all. But he makes it clear that the truce is a tentative one. He tells Caspian he will believe in anyone or anything that will crush the Telmarines and force them to leave Narnia. "Aslan *or* the White Witch, do you understand?" It is interesting that Nikabrik accepts Aslan as long as he seems to be on Nikabrik's and the dwarfs' side. Trumpkin, by contrast, steadfastly refuses to believe in Aslan until he meets him face-to-face. Yet Trumpkin is always faithful to Caspian, while Nikabrik is the vacillator.

Nikabrik refuses to be one of the messengers to go in search of the ancient kings and queens, because he is afraid the dwarfs will be mistreated during his absence. Although there is no reason for him to be suspicious about Caspian's motives, Nikabrik accuses him of putting the dwarfs in the thickest part of the battle.

Nikabrik is corruptible; Trumpkin says that it would never do to let him see the treasure chamber at Cair Paravel. Nikabrik worships power. He does not care where it comes from, as long as it favors the dwarfs.

Nikabrik's struggle with himself comes to a head the night the Pevensies and Trumpkin arrive in camp. Everything had gone wrong that day: The battle plan had been bungled because of the innate stupidity of giants; horrible casualties had been sustained. The hoped-for help from the blowing of Susan's horn appears not to have come.

Food is running short, and the little army is becoming discouraged.

Nikabrik is out of patience and will not die nobly for a just cause, as Trumpkin would gladly do. So Nikabrik goes to the only other source of power he knows: the White Witch. Even as he explains his plan to the others, it is clear he does not like what he is saying. But, as Caspian observes, his hatred and suffering and love of power have finally overcome his better qualities. Nikabrik is clearly affected by paranoia, and he draws smaller and smaller circles around himself and his race, and finally shuts everyone else out.

This kind of behavior is a perfect picture of racial bigotry. Nikabrik fails to see that he really needs the help of beasts and fauns and satyrs and giants and men. His mistrust, instead of protecting him, destroys him; he sourly digs his own grave, as many bigots have done before him.

Most of Lewis's fantasy books offer fascinating portrayals of evil. *Prince Caspian* is no exception. The hag and wer-wolf are reminiscent of the characters of Mr. Wither and Dr. Frost in *That Hideous Strength*. It was Lewis's idea that evil shatters things—breaks them up into their separate components—and that evil tends to take one character trait and exaggerate it to the exclusion of all else. Mr. Wither and the hag represent one tendency of evil: the tendency toward vapid nothingness. Mr. Wither is watery-eyed, is stooped, never looks at anyone, wanders in a daze, never makes any definite statements, and contains no positive qualities. The hag is whiny, apologetic, insinuating, and has the backbone of an eel. In contrast to Mr. Wither and the hag, Dr. Frost and the wer-wolf are alike in their ruthless coldness and in their direct, unrelenting approach to pursuing their evil desires. Dr. Frost has taken logical positivism, with its insistence on verifiable facts, to an extreme. He displays no emotion, insists on scientific rigor in every detail of life, operates like an automaton, has honed his whole personality down to a sharp cutting edge, and brings the chill of a winter wind to those with whom he comes in contact. The wer-wolf is close kin to him in personality, although the motivating characteristic of both, like that of the hag, is hatred. Nikabrik has become his true brother, through the perfection of his hatred. The wer-wolf's boast is that he can impart his hatred to his body, even after death.

While Nikabrik nursed his hatred with the belief that help would not come from Aslan, the help was at the door. With some patience, he could have avoided the downfall that came to him.

The Wild Awakes

There is a strong presence of nature in all the Narnia books, but in *Prince Caspian* it comes bursting to the fore when the land avenges itself against the cruel, destructive reign of Miraz and the Telmarines. Lewis loved nature, and his favorite activity during his younger years was taking walking tours in various parts of England, accompanied by his friends.

Lewis was not a friend of those elements of civilization that destroy the land and its occupants. He was not opposed to taming the land, but he objected strongly to obliterating it in the name of progress. His strongest presentation of this theme occurred in *That Hideous Strength*, where he exposed the fraud of pseudoscience. Because he believed that man could control nature without defacing it, he was comfortable in the manicured setting of an eighteenth-century formal garden as well as in the wild woods of the Romantics.

One of the greatest desecrations committed by the Telmarines was the ravaging of Narnian nature. This action combined the needless destruction of nature with the sin of murder, since in Narnia even the trees have souls. The Telmarines combine disrespect for nature with a fear of it. They cut down as much of the woods as possible and stay away from what remains, which is left as a shield from another natural threat: the sea. The Telmarines have closed themselves in sad little cities full of dull routine. Lewis says that even Telmarine history books (which have been falsified) are duller than any true history.

The naiads and dryads, beings who live in the trees and waters, are moribund but not totally lifeless. They bestir themselves enough to give Caspian a nasty knock on the head as he rides through the woods. Lucy almost calls them to life but cannot quite find the key to doing so. Finally, Aslan brings the trees fully awake to eliminate the rule of the usurper Miraz.

Lewis mixes classical mythology with his story of nature's revenge. Bacchus, Silenus, and the maenads are mysteriously mingled in an unconventional pastoral romp. In mythology, all these characters are rather shady: Bacchus was popularly known as the god of wine and drunkenness; Silenus was Bacchus's foster father and the chief of the satyrs, who were known for their sexual lust; the maenads were the insane women who attended Bacchus. But Lewis cleans up the story. He emphasizes Bacchus's lesser-known function as the god of grapes. Silenus is simply the funny old host who wants everyone to have plenty to eat. Even the maenads are described as being *madcap*, which means "impulsive" and "frolicsome," but not "insane." Lewis has taken the good parts from the old myths and let the rest go.

Susan says, however, that she wouldn't care to meet this wild crew without Aslan, and she is right. Their danger is controlled by the power of God. Lewis might have cited his use of mythological characters as an example of what the apostle Paul meant when he said, "Prove all things; hold fast that which is good" (1 Thess. 5:21 KJV). At any rate, Greek and Roman mythology were a source of inspiration for Lewis, and they provided the impetus that resulted in the Narnia tales.

The Telmarines, in turning their backs on the true king of Narnia, Aslan, have also turned their backs on nature. Aslan is not only the one who makes the rulers;

he is also the one who creates all the good things his creatures enjoy. In turning from him, they have shut out all real life. Christians can enjoy God's creation only as they follow His rules, because without those rules, everything falls apart.

Telmarine civilization goes down in a hurry before the wild party led by Aslan. The river god, who seems like Neptune, is freed from the chains of Beruna Bridge. The destructive force is masses of ivy growing like wildfire. The next object of wild liberation is a Telmarine school featuring straight-laced classes in false Narnian history. The occupants of the school are forced to come out in the light of reality and face up to the existence of creatures they have never dreamed of. One student, Gwendolyn, *has* dreamed, or at least had longings that are fulfilled in her meeting with Aslan. When the group encounters a Telmarine arithmetic class, all the students are confirmed in their piggish nature, but the teacher is shot through with joy at the sight of Aslan. No matter how compromising a person's position may be or how entrenched he or she may be in an evil establishment, God may be dealing with that person, and he or she may be ready to respond to the freedom of His Word.

Even an unwise testimony can receive its reward. Caspian's old nurse, who used to babble about Old Narnia and the talking animals, was not as discreet as Doctor Cornelius, but she planted the first seed of imagination in Caspian, and she receives new life when Aslan shows her that her words were true.

The Narnians and those Telmarines who have unknowingly tried to serve Aslan are freed and remain in Narnia. But the Telmarines who have taken part in the destruction of the country are returned to this world, the place from which they came.

The Narnian nature that the Telmarines so feared has been used by Aslan as a tool in his destruction of their power. When he has placed the proper king on the throne—one who will rule in his name—nature returns to its normal function. There is rejoicing over the newfound freedom of Narnia, and the Pevensies return to their own world, their mission accomplished.

5

The Voyage of the *Dawn Treader*

The Voyage of the Dawn Treader, like all the Narnia books, is an adventure story. Experienced readers of fairy tales will recognize it as belonging to the genre of the quest. The quest involves a great journey into the unknown, against difficult odds, to reach or achieve a specific objective. The journey may be over land or sea or both: Frodo, in J. R. R. Tolkien's *Lord of the Rings*, makes a land journey, spanning three volumes, to destroy the accursed ring of power; in *The Voyage of the* Dawn Treader, the quest is a sea voyage.

Beginning the Quest

The quest normally begins at or near home, in familiar surroundings. This helps the reader identify with those involved in the journey and feel more empathetic, as they move from accustomed circumstances to difficult and dangerous ones. The familiar in this case is the house of Harold and Alberta, the parents of Eustace. The opening scene is commonplace, with Lucy and Edmund unwillingly being sent to the house of their least favorite aunt, uncle, and cousin. But the ordinary quickly fades away as an out-of-place picture suddenly becomes a gateway between this world and Narnia, and Lucy and Edmund and their nasty cousin Eustace are pulled into an ocean voyage with King Caspian.

Every quest has a purpose or objective, and this one is no exception. Caspian explains to Lucy and Edmund that he has sworn an oath to sail eastward a year and a day, in search of seven lords sent away by Caspian's usurping Uncle Miraz. The secondary purpose is that the greatest of the mice, Reepicheep, intends to sail to the eastern end of the world, in search of Aslan's country.

The ship in which Caspian and the others are traveling helps set the mood. It is shaped like a dragon, with green sides and golden trim. It has a purple sail, a huge dragon-headed prow and a tail protruding from the stern. Lewis lovingly describes the *Dawn Treader*, showing how fond he was of ships. He took them many times in his youth, to travel between his home in Northern Ireland and school in England. Lewis's brother, Warren, was even more a fan of sailing craft. Warren was an expert on the French galleons in use during the seventeenth century.

Despite their dunking, seeing the *Dawn Treader* and greeting their old friend Caspian causes the spirit of adventure to rise up in Lucy and Edmund. The challenge of the life of faith can likewise become the believer's adventure.

Cleansing the Augean Stables

The mythical hero Hercules was set the task of performing twelve mighty deeds. One of these deeds was cleansing the Augean stables, which were used by three thousand oxen and were full of incredible filth. He accomplished the deed by redirecting two neighboring rivers through the stables. The Lone Islands have dirt of another kind in them. It's bureaucratic filth that can only be cleansed by extraordinary measures.

The Lone Islands are ruled by a governor whose name is Gumpas. Although Governor Gumpas has pledged fealty to the king of Narnia, Lord Bern informs Caspian that the good governor would not be especially pleased to receive a visit from his distant ruler. In fact, like everything else in the Lone Islands, Gumpas's loyalty to Narnia is a sham. He is dedicated to lining his pockets and those of his friends with ill-gotten gains.

The Lone Islands appear to be an easy realm to rule. They are small, are compact, are temperate, offer good grazing land, and are on established trade routes. They are, in fact, so easy to rule that Gumpas and his underlings have become slovenly and slipshod. They have retreated behind a tangled mass of bureaucratic red tape, confusion, indecision, and endless delay.

The effects of this course of action are always fatal. Charles Dickens shows this in *Little Dorrit* with his bureaucratic caricature, the Circumlocution Office, whose motto is "How not to do it." Those who threaten to do anything for the nation or the people are shunned, despised, delayed, pigeonholed, and finally alienated. Those who can do it must either give it up or do it in some other country.

The Lone Islands are that kind of place. While Gumpas muddles and messes with his accounts and forms and regulations, the slave trade thrives, Gumpas rakes off his share, and the people are left to govern themselves. His rules in themselves are not immoral, but they are being used for evil purposes.

Caspian's approach to the inefficient administration of the Lone Islands is simple and direct. He plays on Gumpas's cowardice to force his way past the guards into his castle, and he throws Gumpas out of office when he refuses to abolish the slave trade. The labyrinth of paperwork behind which the governor has hidden his petty meanness is symbolically cast aside. This is something a king can do on the spot, which may take years in a democracy. In either case, however, the principle is the same: What purpose is being served by the existing system, and is it right?

Caspian turns the tables on Gumpas by requiring compliance with Narnian law and demanding one hundred and fifty years' worth of tribute. When Caspian questions the necessity of the slave trade, Gumpas cites economic factors as justification. Caspian rejoins that the slave trade is not bringing consumable goods into the Lone Islands; what it does bring is monetary gain to the traders and the corrupt administration. Since these people are rich anyway, they probably do not return their tainted gains to the economy of the islands.

But Caspian clinches the matter with his response to Gumpas's question concerning what is to become of progress and development. Caspian answers that he has seen both in the egg: "We call it *Going bad* in Narnia." Progress and change for their own sakes are not enough. Progress must occur toward a desirable and moral goal. Change must be from something bad or indifferent or improvable to something better.

The Saga of Useless Eustace

The most prominent human figure in *The Voyage of the Dawn Treader* is a puny little boy by the name of Eustace Clarence Scrubb. Lewis observes that he almost deserves his name. It is really rather amazing that Lewis could tell such an effective story so nearly concerned with this unprepossessing character. Eustace is a loser. His parents, who expect Eustace to address them by their first name, will do anything to appear "advanced." They are against everything: meat, tobacco, alcohol, furniture, blankets, and closed rooms. Lewis hated claptrap or phoniness of any kind, and Eustace's parents are prime examples of these weaknesses.

Besides his unconventional parents, Eustace has the disadvantage of a modern-school education, where there is no corporal punishment and the emphasis is on economic information rather than the liberal-arts disciplines. Lewis was very much opposed to certain trends in contemporary education. He even wrote a book about it called *The Abolition of Man*. Lewis's main complaint was that the moral content was being drained out of instruction. He felt that this tended to create people with heads but no chests. In other words, children could learn specific information at school, but they were not taught the principles of courage, honesty, and integrity so they could use that information wisely. This is certainly true of Eustace.

Eustace is unable to cope with Narnia when he literally falls into that land. He has not read the sort of literature designed to develop his imagination, so he cannot even comprehend the sorts of things he sees there. The one piece of information he has about how to cope with a foreign country—that is, to contact the British consul—is worthless. He has no moral underpinnings to support him, and he can find no reference point from which to get his bearings. His reaction is to cry like a baby. All in all, Eustace deserves Edmund's description of him as a "record stinker." Edmund also observes, "It only makes him worse if you try to be nice to him."

Eustace's feelings on the voyage are clearly set forth in his diary. His reaction to the *Dawn Treader* is totally negative because it lacks the horsepower, size, and modern conveniences that he admires in British ships.

Besides his tasteless attitude toward everything he sees, Eustace is fond of exaggeration and has a self-seeking spirit that hides behind an avowed sense of what is due to him. These qualities are combined with a paranoia that sees everyone else as "fiend in human form," full of bad motives and ill will toward himself. Fair weather at sea is a "frightful storm" that continually threatens to capsize the ship. Others do not reflect this cowardice, because they insist on ignoring facts. The ship is a "rotten little thing." The cabin he shares with Edmund is a "hole." In fact, Eustace expects this, or any other world, to be an extension of his own personality. Anything unfamiliar or not in accordance with his ideas has no right to exist. He projects his own hatred and bullying characteristics onto those around him. When they appear to treat him kindly, he suspects them of treachery. When they don't share his fears, Eustace assumes that they must be hiding their real trepidation.

Eustace wrongly concludes, after his first scornful glance around the ship, that the most likely candidate for bullying is Reepicheep, the "performing animal." However, his attempts to misuse Reepicheep's tail end in disaster. The little mouse is not as helpless as he appears and, by giving him a good thrashing, teaches Eustace a lesson he never learned at school. Eustace hypocritically combines his bullying ways with a belief in pacifism and an opposition to corporal punishment. Lewis could not stand hypocrisy and did not mind exposing it wherever he encountered it. The belligerency of some modern pacifists struck him as being a contradiction in terms.

The encounter with Reepicheep teaches Eustace nothing except that the mouse is more dangerous than he supposed. Eustace is still scornful of the *Dawn Treader* and brags to Drinian that British ships are so large you don't even realize you're at sea when you're inside. Drinian dryly observes that in that case you might as well stay ashore. When Lucy, Edmund, Eustace, and Caspian are kidnapped by pirates, Eustace blames everyone but himself. He does not even have value as a slave; Pug, the slave trader and pirate, cannot give Eustace away, because he could "talk the hind leg off a donkey." Lewis's picture of Eustace as "a sort of utility slave whom no one will buy" is rather pathetic, but funny.

Eustace's diary resumes after a ruinous storm breaks the mast of the *Dawn Treader* and drives the ship far out to sea. He is forced to do a little manual labor, and, exaggerating as usual, says he has had to "work like a slave." Reepicheep in particular infuriates him, because the mouse possesses the courage Eustace lacks. Eustace must attribute Reepicheep's bravery to a desire to show off. An example of how wrongheaded a person who is above correction can be occurs when Caspian says that his men cannot row the ship on rations of a half-pint of water per day. Eustace insists that this is wrong, because rowing will cause the men to perspire, which will cool them down. What he fails to realize is that moisture lost through perspiration must be replaced by liquid intake, or the body will become overheated. Eustace further displays his dog-in-the-manger attitude by criticizing Caspian's decision to sail on after the storm, although Eustace cannot propose an alternative plan. He even has the nerve to call sailing on an instance of wishful thinking.

The ultimate in self-concern masquerading as innocence is displayed when Eustace sneaks out of his cabin in search of a drink of water. When challenged by Reepicheep, who is guarding the water casks, Eustace fabricates a story about wanting to go on deck. He justifies his lie to himself on the grounds that Reepicheep does not need to know that he requires water. Everyone sees through his lies, and Caspian threatens to punish the next person caught stealing water. Eustace takes this as an example of Caspian's tyranny. When Caspian tries to sympathize with him, Eustace dismisses his words as patronizing.

Eustace is obviously in need of a dramatic experience to shock his attention away from his own selfish concerns, and he gets it at the first land past the Lone Islands that the party encounters. As usual, Eustace is busy being lazy. He has been forced to do a little physical labor on board ship, and he is anxious to avoid doing more, now that the party is ashore. So he decides to sneak away, climb a nearby ridge, and take a nap. His attempts to escape work cause much more exertion in climbing the ridge than would have been required back in camp, but he struggles on nevertheless.

Once he attains his objective, Eustace discovers he is lonely for practically the first time in his life. This feeling may seem a bit out of character for Eustace, until you realize that even though he is full of hatred and spite, he has almost always been around other people. Without knowing it, he feeds off their presence, even while he is berating them. He is so void of good characteristics that he is not self-sustaining. When all outside influences are gone, he has only his miserable self to contemplate, and not even Eustace can tolerate that.

Eustace's encounter with the dragon is his meeting with destiny. The dragon represents the fruition of Eustace's chosen lifestyle. The dragon is free to be as selfish as he pleases. He has no natural enemies and can loot, pillage, destroy, and hoard to his heart's content, without significant fear of reprisal. He need not even attempt to get along with his own kind and can watch over his worthless treasure as long as his internal fire lasts. As Lewis observes, Eustace should not have been surprised to awaken as a dragon, after sleeping on a dragon's hoard with greedy thoughts inside. His grasping childhood has been a perfect preparation for a dragonish adulthood.

His dragon shape helps Eustace see himself and others in a proper light. Although his little ploys have fooled no one else, he has succeeded in pulling the wool over his own eyes. Now that he really is a beast, he can see that his companions were not such monsters after all. When he has the power to destroy them, he no longer cares to. He is experiencing remorse for his actions for the first time.

The dragon Eustace has the mind of a little boy but the body and desires of a dragon. He becomes physically insensitive to the sharp gems and crowns in his hoard.

He gobbles up the dead dragon before he realizes it. He runs on all fours, flies, and devours raw meat without thinking about it. But his dragonish claws do not know how to write a message in the sand. Although he knows how to act like a dragon, the mind of Eustace finds the whole thing unspeakably dreary. His only real pleasure consists of helping the others—by killing wild goats and swine, serving as a heating pad for the party, starting fires, and finding a new mast for the *Dawn Treader*.

The others are immediately aware of the change in Eustace and respond to it. Those he thought were his greatest enemies become his best friends. In fact, they were acting as well toward him as they could before, but he had never before been receptive to their advances. Now that he sees the truth about himself, he is free to discover the truth about others. He discovers that he has always been an unmitigated burden to them.

Now that he recognizes his need for deliverance inwardly and outwardly, all that is lacking is a real conversion from a self-directed life to one that revolves around his Maker; this occurs when Eustace meets Aslan. At first, all Eustace wants to do is soothe his aching arm by bathing it in the pool to which Aslan leads him. But Aslan tells him he must undress first. So Eustace tries to obey. Three times he scratches off his skin, and three times he discovers that he is still hard and scaly.

. Man is doomed to failure when he tries to shed his own sinfulness. The stain goes too deep and he is too kind to himself to cut to the quick in removing his evil traits. Only God and His Word can penetrate to the dividing asunder of soul and spirit. Finally, Eustace must admit that he cannot save himself and submits his dragonish body to Aslan's claws. Aslan scratches Eustace much deeper than he would have thought possible, and that scratch hurts much more than Eustace would have thought he could stand. (Eustace tells us his own scratches didn't hurt.) But then, Eustace has underestimated the depth of his scaly skin. Now that it is off, he is thrown into the cleansing pool and becomes Eustace the little boy again. But he has new clothes and a new heart.

In order to be changed by Aslan, Eustace must turn belly up, opening himself to the pain he fears. It is only desperation that drives him to this, and he says, "It hurts like billy-oh." Here is a picture of the confession of sin. Confession may at first appear to be impossible for the believer, but it is the only way to find release.

Eustace is no model of virtue after his conversion, but he does show marked improvement. Things like rainy weather and a lost game of chess still get him down, but there is a new resiliency to his spirit. He bounces back from a display of irritability to engage in his first brave action. With a borrowed sword, he attacks a sea serpent that has surrounded the *Dawn Treader*. His deed is foolish, since the sea serpent is impervious to attack, but his act is motivated by a sincere desire to help. As Lewis says, "It was a fine thing for a beginner to have done."

The Noble Mouse

If Eustace is the human focal point of *The Voyage of the Dawn Treader*, then Reepicheep is its heart. Reepicheep's courage is the wind that keeps the sails of the ship filled and moving forward. Many times, when even Caspian is reluctant to go on or hesitant about the right course of action, Reepicheep is there recommending and even insisting on the boldest alternative. He is not always right, but his presence is a constant inspiration to the passengers and crew of the adventure ship.

Lewis gives a vivid description of the greatest of the mice. He is two feet tall, nearly black, wearing a long sword and having round his head a thin band of gold that holds a red feather. Reepicheep is comfortable in all circumstances. Though he is a land creature, he maintains perfect balance on board ship. He is never abashed by a threatened peril. He simply seeks the bravest response and acts accordingly. When the *Dawn Treader* is shot at by pirates, he feels the ship should give chase to the pirate ship and hang every one of the miscreants. Even though the ship's company experiences several adventures between Narnia and the Lone Islands, the mouse indicates that the real adventures lie beyond, in the uncharted sea.

With all his warlike ways, Reepicheep is the most courteous of beings. He greets Lucy with gallant words and a deep bow. He is formal and polite even to his enemies. This comes through clearly in his initial encounters with Eustace. When Eustace wails about the vulgarity of performing animals, Reepicheep is offended, but accuses Eustace of nothing worse than discourtesy. The strongest word that Reepicheep uses in berating anyone is *poltroon*. Since cowardice is the worst of all sins to Reepicheep, *poltroon* has a very serious connotation for him.

Surprisingly, there is a poetic side to Reepicheep's nature. The verse a dryad spoke to him when he was a baby mouse haunts him all his life. It gives him a deep longing for the eastern seas and promises fulfillment for all his inward desires. It is this voyage that will enable him to unravel the meaning of that verse and appreciate the true significance of his life. The incredible courage he possesses is a necessary quality for meeting his destiny in the utter east.

The moment of truth between Eustace and Reepicheep, when that cowardly boy discovers that the mouse cannot be bullied, emphasizes several characteristics of Reepicheep's nature. He is caught off guard, and Eustace has him at a complete disadvantage, but his balance, presence of mind, and fencing ability result in his quick release. Reepicheep wants to fight a duel but has an unwilling opponent. So he does the next best thing. He soothes his honor by giving Eustace an old-fashioned thrashing with his sword. When Eustace runs to Caspian, Edmund, and Lucy to tattle, the mouse is fiercely polite and apologetic. He is not sorry to have taught Eustace a badly needed lesson, but he is sorry to have disturbed the two kings and the queen. Although Reepicheep is a hothead, he always manages to maintain control.

Another side of Reepicheep's nature is emphasized in the encounter with the slavers. He is ready to fight Pug and his thugs, but Caspian counsels caution. When Caspian and his companions are captured, Reepicheep fights with everything he has. He bites until he must either stop or be muzzled. Then he spews out a steady stream of invective against his captors. Their attitude toward him is similar to Eustace's first reaction: The talking mouse is a curiosity—something to be caged and displayed at shows. He is considered to be subhuman—not really rational. His ability to talk is a trick of imitation, like a parrot's—something he has been taught by the others.

This condescending attitude infuriates Reepicheep more than anything else could. He does not mind being mistreated nearly as much as he does being ignored and looked down upon. In *Prince Caspian*, Lewis shows that the sense of his own dignity is one of the strongest features in the makeup of the mouse. He knows he is small and is constantly ready to use his sword to prove he is as good as anyone. Being caged and laughed at is the one thing that might break his spirit and diminish the courage of the noble mouse.

The effect that Reepicheep has on the others can be seen in Caspian's response to Lord Bern's request that he stay in the Lone Islands. Caspian reminds Bern that he has sworn an oath to discover the fate of the six other lords who sailed from Narnia. "And anyway, what *could* I say to Reepicheep?" the king asks.

The mouse's valiant nature even comes through in the way he plays chess. He is intelligent enough to play the game well, but every once in a while he forgets that it is a game. Then he reacts as he would in a war and makes brash moves that are doomed to failure. Lewis tells us that "his mind was full of forlorn hopes, death or glory charges, and last stands."

Reepicheep's relations with Eustace on Dragon Island reveal the best side of the mouse's character. Even though Eustace thinks the "Mouse thing" is a show-off, Reepicheep is prepared to get along with him, provided Eustace does not insult Reepicheep's honor. When Eustace disappears after the ship puts ashore, Reepicheep criticizes Drinian for saying good riddance to their troublesome shipmate. Reepicheep avows that he and Eustace are not friends, but Eustace is a relative of Queen Lucy, and it is their duty to find Eustace and avenge him if he has been killed.

When the dragon Eustace appears, Reepicheep is ready to take him on in single combat, not knowing who he is. Caspian squelches that idea by threatening to tie up Reepicheep. When they confront the dragon and he acts strangely, Reepicheep addresses the dragon and learns that he cannot talk but does understand speech. After it becomes known that the dragon is Eustace, the mouse is his greatest comforter. He spends hours sitting to the windward side of the dragon's head, telling him about the turn of fortune's wheel, which may take him from the depths of despair to the height of prosperity.

(This is the Narnian middle ages, and the turn of fortune's wheel was one of the great literary themes of the medieval period.)

Reepicheep's devotion to courage is not a blind thing. He shows that he is able to use his head and keep his heroic impulses under control in the encounter with the sea serpent. Eustace ruins Caspian's second-best sword, hacking away at the serpent, but Reepicheep realizes it is futile to fight the creature, which is looping itself around the *Dawn Treader* with the intention of tightening the loop and snapping the ship to bits. So Reepicheep suggests pushing against the serpent and forcing the ship out of the fatal loop. He shoves until he is exhausted, and the others take over.

Reepicheep's courage is not limited to enemies he can see. When the company is threatened by the invisible Duffers, he says that it is as well to face up to invisible forces, since it is impossible to hide from or avoid them. This time, the bravest course of action is the best, and the others take his advice. But when it appears their only chance of escaping is for Lucy to sneak upstairs in the magician's house to find the spell for making invisible things visible, Reepicheep unexpectedly supports her decision to attempt the deed. His reasons for making this change are that they really have no chance against the Duffers; there is a chance of Lucy succeeding; and it is a noble undertaking that will not demean her.

Not only is Reepicheep unafraid of invisible foes, he does not fear darkness itself. Everyone is willing to turn away from Dark Island, except Reepicheep. He castigates the others for not wanting to pursue such a great adventure. They reluctantly give in, after making a few comments about the mouse's view of honor. When the hysterical Lord Rhoop screams out to them in the darkness, Reepicheep is the only one with the courage to respond. Finally, Rhoop informs them that this is the island where dreams come true. After Rhoop makes the others fully aware of the significance of that fact, there is a mad dash to escape the darkness. Reepicheep again accuses the others of poltroonery, but this time he is ignored. Caspian informs him that there are certain things no man can face. Reepicheep strikes the final blow for his valor, despite his diminutive size, when he says, "It is, then, my good fortune not to be a man."

It should be clear by this time what a splendid character Lewis has created in this noble mouse. Reepicheep very nearly steals *Prince Caspian*, and there is no question who commands our attention in *The Voyage of the Dawn Treader*.

The Art of Contentment

Lewis addresses the problem of contentment in the Christian life in two episodes of *The Voyage of the Dawn Treader*. The first incident occurs on the island Reepicheep calls Deathwater. Here Caspian, Eustace, Lucy, Edmund, and Reepicheep decide to explore and climb to the headwaters of the second of two streams they had seen flowing into the sea. After discovering a dead Lord Restimar, the truth slowly dawns on them that this water turns anything to gold. Suddenly Caspian is no longer content with his kingdom. He wants to be that world's richest king. Edmund is also affected. He does something he has never thought of doing before on this trip—exercising his authority, as an ancient king of Narnia, over Caspian. They always complemented each other perfectly before, but the magic word *gold* puts them at each other's throats. Even Lucy is drawn in. She does not want the gold, but she does speak uncharacteristically of Caspian and Edmund as "swaggering, bullying idiots."

This is an extreme temptation—one that is irresistible to those confronted by it. This presents an interesting problem. The apostle Paul says in 1 Corinthians 10:13 that the believer will not be tempted beyond his ability to resist, yet who can say no to unlimited wealth? The solution in this case is direct intervention by Aslan himself. He gets them through the crucial moment by confusing their minds with partial amnesia. They forget most of what has occurred in the last few hours and remember only that this is a deadly island that should be avoided at all costs.

Not satisfied with the lesson in contentment on Deathwater Island, Lewis next introduces the Duffers. These humorous little people are very stupid; they are very cowardly; they are very conceited. And they are blind to the defects of their Chief, whose every word they dote upon. But there is much they should be thankful for. They live on a beautiful, temperate, well-groomed island, with plenty of the good things in life to enjoy. The broad, immaculate lawns, neatly spaced trees, weedless walks, and fine old country homes represent the sort of England Lewis loved. It is somewhat like the universities of Oxford and Cambridge, where Lewis spent most his life. All that is lacking are a few grazing deer to complete the scene Lewis saw many times from the windows of his rooms in college.

Not only do the Duffers have a beautiful environment in which to live; they also have a very wise, kind, and patient master, though they cannot appreciate him. The magician who rules this island must use "rough magic" to keep the Duffers in line, only because they will not learn how to care for themselves. Magic in this case is obviously not the desirable way to accomplish things. It is a stopgap measure to keep the island's economy from falling apart. The magician would love to lock up his magic book and simply instruct the Duffers in daily living, but the Duffers will not submit to him. Even tasks like cutting the lawn and raking the leaves are probably accomplished by magic, since the Duffers are too busy feeling sorry for themselves because they have been "uglified" and made invisible. Someday the Duffers must learn that cutting the grass yourself makes you much more appreciative of the lawn than letting a magician do it behind your back.

The Duffers' very stupidity makes a direct approach through their reason extremely difficult. Their entire

speech consists of agreements and tautological statements: Water is wet, night is dark, invisible things can't be
seen, and so on. While these statements are, by definition,
true, they say nothing. They do not lead to the association
of ideas or the introduction of new knowledge. Stating
that white is white and black is black tells nothing about
the relationship of white to black. So far, the Duffers have
not learned the basic principles of Aristotelian logic, one
of which is that a thing cannot be its opposite. When
Lucy and the Chief Monopod make opposite statements
to the Duffers, they agree with both.

Even though the Duffers despise the wise magician
and love their conceited and wrongheaded Chief, the
magician does not wish to take away their respect for the
Chief Monopod. The magician opines that their admiring him is preferable to their admiring no one. Some
of the Duffers' admiration for their Chief is shifted to
the little girl who makes them visible. When she tells
them they are not ugly, they do not disagree with their
Chief, who claims they are still ugly, but they appear to
be contented with their lot. Their contentment grows
when Reepicheep shows them how to turn their peculiar
single foot into a raft.

Lucy receives her own lesson in contentment. She is
really the key figure on the island of the Duffers, because
she is the one who must restore the situation to normal
and bring the Duffers out of their unproductive, invisible state into a condition where they can slowly progress
toward responsibility. She is barely equal to the situa-

tion. The temptation for her to become the world's most beautiful woman (and cause the world to go to war over her) is equivalent to Caspian's temptation to become the richest king. But although Caspian must be rescued from his temptation by amnesia, Lucy, as the most devoted of Aslan's servants, is not tempted beyond her ability to withstand. But in the end it is her fear of Aslan rather than her love that makes her turn the page. Perfect love casts out fear and makes it unnecessary, but unfortunately Lucy's love is not quite perfect.

Lucy compensates for passing up the big sin by committing one with more limited, but still painful, consequences. In Aslan's words, she eavesdrops on one of her friends. As a result, she is hurt and may even lose a friend, if she cannot overcome her reaction. There is nothing like a series of small sins to create discontent.

Once Lucy repents of her double-mindedness, her equilibrium and good humor are restored. One more element assists in her recovery—the story she loves so much, but cannot remember. The story is, of course, an account of Jesus' crucifixion and resurrection. The cup is the cup of sorrows that Jesus had to drink in Gethsemane and on the cross. The sword is the one Peter used to cut off the ear of the high priest's servant. The tree is the one that became the cross and had to be carried by Jesus to the scene of His crucifixion. The green hill is either the hill of Golgotha where the crucifixion occurred or perhaps the one where all the disciples were gathered when Jesus ascended into heaven. Aslan informs Lucy that he will be telling her the story all of her life. It is through that story that she may overcome discontent.

Aslan's Table

Sailing from the island of the Duffers to the island of Aslan's Table is like moving from one world into another. To be more precise, it is a journey from the fringes of the Narnian world to the fringes of Aslan's own country. The sun becomes imperceptibly larger. New constellations appear in the sky. The waves gradually subside, and the little company feels as if they are sailing on a lake rather than the sea. An aura of peace begins to descend on the *Dawn Treader*. The noise and battle of earth are giving way to the calm and tranquillity of heaven.

In our world one gets to heaven not by traveling but by believing. In Narnia the same is true, but Lewis's model teaches a lesson. Though it may not be part of the visible universe, heaven is only a heartbeat away from any Christian. It is not unattainable, and it is not totally removed from man. The Holy Spirit is the link to that world of joy and tranquillity. In a sense, heaven can be traveled to. The journey begins at salvation, and as long as he follows the Lord's footsteps, the believer finds himself drawing closer and closer to His heavenly realm. Soon, the streets and hills begin to display God's glory. For those saints well on the way, nearly every created thing that still retains some goodness or purity hints of the destination: paradise.

The landing party at the little island recognizes at once that there is a strange character to the place. Everything they see reeks of deep magic. The pillars surrounding Aslan's Table and covered by nothing but sky are reminders of the ruined castle of Cair Paravel in *Prince Caspian* and the ruins of Tintern Abbey, which Lewis loved so much. This setting combines the beauty of architecture, the holiness of a place of worship, and the freshness of the out-of-doors.

Even at the gateway to Aslan's country, sin has left its mark. The stone knife used by the White Witch to kill Aslan has been brought here as a memorial, but one of the three Narnian lords who had sailed thus far seized it to use in a murderous attack. The knife cast a sleeping spell on all three. It is as though the cross, after Christ died on it, were used to crucify other victims. Perhaps a closer parallel can be drawn to Old Testament Israel's ark of the covenant, which meant death if it were touched by the nonpriestly Jew. The idea was that the ark signified the presence of God and could not be approached by those who were unworthy. God often takes common things and blesses them to a sacred use. Examples are the bread and the wine in the sacrament of communion. But He does not appreciate man taking sacred things and cheapening or defiling them. Making a trade fair out of the temple especially displeased Him, and He is not happy when believers falsely swear an oath "by heaven" or "by all that's holy" or use His name in vain.

It is interesting that the voyagers are so heedless about getting into trouble in the Lone Islands and are so careful on this island, controlled by Aslan, that they will not eat the feast spread for them. True, they have had some harrowing experiences to teach them respect for the unknown, and this country is unfamiliar to them. But they have also had enough contact with Aslan to begin to sense when he is present. In other words, some of them, perhaps Lucy, should have known that the strange magic, in this case, is good magic.

When all the others are afraid to taste of the feast spread before them, Reepicheep comes through with his most endearing action. The noble mouse asks Caspian to fill his cup with wine, holds the golden cup with his paws, and says to Ramandu's daughter, "Lady, I pledge you." Then he quaffs his draught and begins to gorge himself on cold peacock. His example soon encourages the others to forget their scruples and partake.

The Voyage of the Dawn Treader has one of the few romantic-love encounters in the Narnia tales, and it is between Caspian and Ramandu's daughter. When he faces the problem of awakening the three sleepers, Caspian states, not too innocently, that in the Pevensies' world the prince had to kiss the princess to dissolve the enchantment. Ramandu's daughter reverses the story: She says that here the king must dissolve the enchantment to kiss the princess. She has, in effect, proposed to him. Caspian is eager to be off and promises to have words with her upon his return.

There are so many symbols toward the end of *The Voyage of the* Dawn Treader that it is difficult to sort them all out.

What, for example, do the birds signify that eat up the unused food every morning at Aslan's Table? Their whiteness probably represents purity and cleanliness. Beyond that, it is not surprising that Aslan would have a completely natural sanitation system. Nothing is wasted. When the primary purpose of feeding the ship's crew is partially frustrated, the secondary purpose of satisfying the birds can still be met. The birds also, in a sense, bring the morning. It is like experiencing the exuberance of a fresh, sunny summer morning and feeling one could almost hear the creation singing a paean of praise to God. At Aslan's Table the song is audible. As the travelers move closer to Aslan's country, the songs of the birds begin to fit into a pattern. Lewis calls it the great dance. Even the stars in Narnia participate in this ordered movement in honor of their maker.

The birds bring personal renewal as well as natural sanitation. A fireberry from the valleys of the sun is brought to Ramandu every morning. Each fireberry takes away a little of his age. This episode is reminiscent of Isaiah's vision of the Lord in the temple (Isaiah 6). Isaiah is so abashed by his own unworthiness that he cries out he is a man of unclean lips dwelling among a people of unclean lips. The Lord's solution is to send one of the seraphim with a hot burning coal to touch Isaiah's lips; the coal burns away his sinfulness. Purification from the world's dross is a daily necessity. Lewis's image is an apt illustration of this fact.

When it is time to leave Aslan's Table, Caspian cannot force his men to go to the world's end, so he offers them a choice of going or staying on the island. When some are reluctant to sail farther, he presents the situation in a different light. It is not an onerous duty to tread the dawn; it is a privilege to be given only those who are truly willing. Reepicheep leads the way with a simple yet powerful statement of intent. He is headed east, whether the ship takes him there or not. While the ship is headed east, he will ride her. When the ship can no longer serve him, his coracle must do. When the coracle sinks, he must swim. "And when I can swim no longer, if I have not reached Aslan's country, or shot over the edge of the world in some vast cataract, I shall sink with my nose to the sunrise and Peepiceek will be head of the talking mice in Narnia." Ultimately, only one sailor is left behind, and he is miserable.

The way Caspian treats the crew of the *Dawn Treader* is a reflection of the way God treats man. If one chooses to follow Him so far but no farther, He allows him to adopt a convenient stopping-off point. But a man should not blame God if he is not altogether happy in his chosen pigeonhole. The sailor who is left behind is lonely, gets rained on, and is totally out of place at Aslan's Table with Ramandu and his daughter. He eventually deserts and flees to the pagan country of Calormen.

Last Things

When the company on the *Dawn Treader* leaves Ramandu and his daughter behind and sails into the last sea, there is a qualitative difference in their lives. The sun becomes overpoweringly large and bright, the sea is like glass and clear to the bottom, and everyone becomes very quiet and wakeful. The necessities of life begin to slip away. When Reepicheep falls into the water after trying to challenge fierce-looking warriors that live under the sea, he discovers that the water is sweet. This fulfills part of the prophecy spoken by the dryad, and he knows his journey is near an end. After that, they all live on seawater. It satisfies them so that they no longer need to eat or sleep; it enables them to bear and utilize incredible amounts of light; and it makes them even quieter and more contemplative. They are not acting now so much as submitting to their fate. And they no longer need to think about their course of action. It is obvious to all of them. The vitalizing water tastes unbearably strong, but they want to keep on drinking it.

The transition from an earthly world to a heavenly one is almost complete. They are no longer living as ordinary creatures, trying to see through the darkness, beset by seemingly insurmountable obstacles, striving to hear the still small voice of their Maker. They have come out of the obscurity of a sinful world into the clarity of an undefiled paradise. The water they drink represents fellowship with the Holy Spirit and feeding on the spiritual food He provides. On a diet like that, who needs ordinary fare? The sun represents the glory of the Son. This whole section is a dramatic illustration of the truth of Jesus' words,

"Man shall not live by bread alone, but by every word that proceeds from the mouth of God" (Matt. 4:4).

Yet even on the doorstep of paradise, sin is possible. Caspian wants to leave his ship behind and go east into Aslan's county with Reepicheep. When the others resist him, he flies into a rage. It is not until he considers the beautiful princess he is to marry and is corrected by Aslan that he comes to his senses. Caspian's sin is wanting too much. There is evidence that the apostle Paul faced the same temptation to remain in heaven when he was taken up into the third heaven. It is so glorious there that he did not want to return to his duty on earth. He tells the Philippians, "For to me to live is Christ, and to die is gain. . . . I am hard pressed between the two. My desire is to depart and be with Christ, for that is far better. But to remain in the flesh is more necessary on your account" (Phil. 1:21, 23–24). Paul overcomes his temptation, and so does Caspian. Caspian returns to a full and happy life in Narnia. He may not be as transcendently happy in Narnia as in Aslan's country, but even the enjoyment of paradise is diminished somewhat by the knowledge that instead of finishing the race one has dropped out after the first lap.

After the party splits up, the remainder of the book is like a dream. The little boat floating silently over a sea of lilies finally brings them to a brief vision of the incredible heights of Aslan's country and to a farewell to a quiveringly joyous mouse. The final scene with the lamb who becomes the lion Aslan for the first time ties together Aslan of Narnia with Christ.

This scene is strongly reminiscent of the episode in John 21 after Jesus' resurrection, when He meets the disciples by the Sea of Galilee. In both instances, the disciples are passing out of a phase where the physical presence of their leader has been much with them into one where they will have only spiritual contact. And in both cases parting instructions are given by the sea, around a meal of fish prepared over an open fire, by the leader. Jesus' disciples are sad because they know He is going away. Edmund and Lucy are concerned because they do not see Aslan in our world. After Jesus tells Peter he will die a violent death, Peter is worried that John may be left on earth till Christ's return. Jesus tells him not to worry about John. In like fashion, Aslan tells Edmund and Lucy they will not return to Narnia. When they ask whether Eustace will return, Aslan questions their need to know the answer.

The purpose for physically leaving the disciples is similar in both cases, too. Jesus wants to go away so the Comforter can come and teach the disciples to walk by faith, and not by sight. Aslan does not want Edmund and Lucy to return to Narnia because they must grow close to their world now and learn to worship Aslan in his earthly manifestation. His appearance as a lamb is the first clue to that identity. Apparently they have not been taught who Jesus really is. But the God who sent them to Narnia can also ensure that they are properly informed of His coming to earth.

6

The Silver Chair

Several of the Narnia books feature a spiritual conversion. In *The Lion, the Witch and the Wardrobe*, it is Edmund's conversion from treachery against his sisters and brother to acceptance of Aslan's sacrifice for him. In *Prince Caspian*, it is the faithful skeptic, Trumpkin, who learns to believe in an elusive lion who is very real. *The Voyage of the* Dawn Treader shows a scrubby Eustace what he is really like and creates the desire to escape from dragonish behavior. *The Silver Chair* also features a conversion, but it is over almost instantaneously. Eustace Scrubb's schoolmate, Jill, goes through all the thoughts and emotions of a nonbeliever being exposed to the claims of Christ and taking her first step of faith, but she has done so by the end of the second chapter.

Jill's conversion begins, as so many do, with a desperate situation. She is an oppressed student within the lawlessness of Experiment House. There is no control over the students, so the bullies among them are free to exercise a dictatorship of the proletariat, complete with informers, purges, and swift and arbitrary judgment for those who are never in favor or fall out of favor. And, of course, the whole thing is done in the name of democracy and enlightenment. Once again, Lewis's views on education and how it is being mismanaged in modern schools come to the fore. His theme is that moral instruction and control are a necessary part of the educational process. When they are ignored, the result is that evil tendencies of human nature, even in children, are free to set up something that is very much like a modern communist state, with the bullies as leaders and the administrators as dupes.

Harried into Heaven

Jill has apparently just been roughed up by "Them." She is crying behind the gym when an unspectacular evangelist named Eustace Scrubb appears on the scene. He will never fill the kingdom, but he does manage to communicate his faith to Jill. He insensitively starts by almost running her down. Then he looks at her face and knows something is wrong. Fortunately, Jill does not keep her feelings inside, and Eustace gets a clue about what is really bothering her. He has the same problem she does: the bullies. This creates a bond between them that would never have existed had Eustace had the easy time of it, which many Christians expect in their lives. Eustace's struggle with the bullies later becomes a useful part of his witness to Jill.

Eustace's next step is a false one. He begins to deliver a sermon in sententious tones. Jill will have none of it. She has heard that tone before and wrongly concludes that Eustace wants her to submit to the status quo. Her challenge puts him on the defensive, and he launches into a recital of his good works since his own conversion. This is too much for Jill, and she begins to cry again.

After beginning so badly, Eustace makes a very wise move. He attends to Jill's immediate emotional needs by offering her a peppermint. She is overwrought by the trauma of her situation and needs something to divert her attention long enough to recover her equilibrium. The peppermint is perfect, because it keeps her busy and affords her pleasure while she is controlling herself. He is showing concern for her physical and emotional needs, which is part of what Christianity is all about. There is no mention in the parable of the Good Samaritan of a tract being included with the money given to the innkeeper. Yet a man is more apt to respond to the good news of Christ after seeing His love in action.

When Jill has recovered enough to be curious about the change that really has occurred in Eustace's life, he becomes very closemouthed about the details. He has to talk himself into entrusting her with the story. The reason, of course, is that what he is telling her is absolute heresy to everything that is taught or believed at Experiment

House. He is offering her fantastic creatures in another world. Experiment House majors in trivialities and meanness and abnormal psychology, and nothing could be less welcome than an old-fashioned fairy tale, full of mystery and adventure.

Eustace is rather embarrassed as he tells his story, and it is not too hard for us to understand why. He fears that Jill's reaction may be similar to that of many persons who hear the gospel for the first time: scathing denial of any possibility of its truth. The idea that God could take on human form is easy to believe, but the record in Matthew and Luke that He allowed Himself to be born ignobly, to live humbly and without honor, to die shamefully for mankind, to rise from the tomb, and to ascend into heaven is, to say the least, beyond the bounds of the world's normal expectations.

Jill is nearly ready to believe Eustace, however, when an ugly thought grips her: What if he is teasing or lying to her? Reinforcing her idea is the numbing presence of a dull, drippy sky and her defeated outlook at Experiment House. She begins to despair. Whenever the surroundings are gloomy or things have been going badly for the Christian, it is easy to believe things have always been this way and will always continue to be this way. It is a frequent theme in *The Silver Chair*.

Jill is still willing to try to escape the pervasive now, however, and she and Eustace discuss the best way to do this. They consider the possibility of using magic to force an entry into Narnia but wisely reject this plan, because

Eustace knows that Aslan does not let others force their will on him. He is the king and is always ready to listen to petitions, but he is not a tame lion to be led about by the whims of his followers. So Eustace decides instead simply to ask Aslan if they can come to his country. Lewis is picturing the attitude the believer should have toward God's will: Man cannot force Him to his will, and frustration will be the result of any attempts to do so.

Jill and Eustace begin to pray to be sent into Narnia, but before they finish, their pursuers are after them. They scramble toward the only possible way of escape they know—the door to the moor. This familiar door becomes a door into another world. Jill is reluctant to pass through but is frightened into doing so by the voices behind her. They are, literally, harried into heaven.

Heaven, as Lewis describes it here, is a rather interesting place. More than anything, it is like a park, full of well-spaced trees, level turf, and brilliantly colored birds who make what first sounds like noise but turns out to be rather advanced music. The music of the birds is heard against a background of profound silence. The impression Lewis gives is of a beautiful, peaceful, and spacious place set on a very high mountain. But the forest seems lonely. Without the presence of Aslan, all the beauty is for naught. The essence of heaven is that God is fully revealed there. Without His presence, heaven would be as lonely as this beautiful park.

Before Jill and Eustace have been five minutes in paradise, however, disaster happens. They come to the edge of a cliff, and Jill tries to show Eustace how good she is in high places. Lewis was fond of pointing out that heaven is not enough to turn bad people into good ones. In *The Great Divorce*, he sends a busload of unrepentant sinners from hell to heaven, and, after being there awhile, almost all are ready to return. The fact is that heaven is not a comfortable place, unless you are committed to its Lord.

Eustace tries to save Jill from falling over the cliff but is himself thrown off. Jill is amazed to see a huge lion rush out of the woods and blow Eustace away from the cliff. It is all frightening for her. Jill tries to rationalize her behavior and blame the whole incident on Eustace for bringing her to this strange land without warning, but it is no good. She remembers Eustace's scream and starts crying. At this point she seems to be really sorry for what she has done.

A Drink of Water

Finally, Jill is cried out and becomes aware of a great thirst. Her whole motivation is to quench that thirst. She becomes aware of a small persistent noise that sounds like water and wanders toward it. When she finds the bright, tempting stream, there is one big obstacle to quenching her thirst—the lion.

The dilemma of the non-Christian is described in this passage. Jill is aware of her need. She knows her situation at Experiment House is desperate. She can find no way of escape for herself. She also knows she is a sinner. She has, as far as she knows, destroyed Eustace through her own foolish pride. And she is terribly thirsty. She needs the water of life that can quench thirst once and for all, as Jesus tells the Samaritan woman, but the water does not come without the water giver. The world would love to quench its thirst, but it cannot do so until it comes in humility to Jesus to receive the water of life. Most people choose to die of thirst instead. Fortunately for her, Jill chooses otherwise.

She is rather cagey about her acceptance, however. When she sees the lion, she is afraid to move or say anything. When Aslan tells her she may drink, she still holds back; she asks him to go away, but he will not leave. She asks him if he will not hurt her if she comes, but he will not promise. Then she asks whether he makes it a habit to eat boys and girls, and he answers that he has swallowed whole realms. When she says she can't come, he tells her that she will die of thirst unless she does. While she is considering the possibility of finding another stream, he tells her there is no other stream.

The world is always looking for another stream. Jesus offers the water of life, but people for the most part do not want it on His terms. They know they are dying of thirst, and at certain times they suspect there may be something to Christianity, but the price is too high. Whosoever will may come and drink of the water of life freely, but he must do so on God's terms. He cannot go away while a man quenches his thirst, because He is the water of life. And He will not promise to limit His impact on a man's life. One must be willing or be willing to be made willing to give up his whole life when he comes to God. He may suffer as a result, but at least his thirst has been quenched. The world may continue to look for other streams, but all they will find will be dry riverbeds where the Lord has moved before or perhaps a few drops scattered around in music, art, literature, or creation, which are intended to give a taste of the real thing and lead man to the streams of living water.

At last Jill drinks, and her thirst is quenched at once. She had been considering taking a quick slurp and running away, but she decides that might be the most dangerous thing of all to do. Jill does not taste and retreat. She drinks and comes to the lion to confess her sin of pride in causing Eustace to fall over the cliff. Jill has been redeemed in the biblical sense of the word.

Aslan tells Jill he has called her and Eustace into his world for a purpose. Jill is puzzled and reminds Aslan that they asked to come. But he says that they would not have called on him unless he had been calling them. The words are the same as Jesus' words when He tells the believer that he or she has not chosen Him, but God has chosen the believer. Aslan has brought them to Narnia to do a job, and that task is the theme of *The Silver Chair*.

The Cheerful Voice of Doom

Like *The Voyage of the* Dawn Treader, *The Silver Chair* relates the story of a perilous journey in the world of

Narnia. The two earth children are commissioned by Aslan to find the missing Prince Rilian. The guide who takes them through the wilderness beyond Narnia is one of Lewis's greatest creations: Puddleglum. He seems a strange choice. He can be very depressing to talk to, but he has qualities Jill and Eustace learn to appreciate by the end of their adventure.

There are abundant examples in this book of Puddleglum's negativism. When the owls first bring Jill and Eustace to him, he is sure that they are bringing news of the king's death or of some calamity that has come to Narnia. He is concerned for the welfare of his young guests but tells them he is sure they will be cold, uncomfortable, and sleepless in his wigwam, that he will not be able to catch a meal for them, that they will fail in trying to start a fire, and that they will dislike his food or get sick on it. All of these dire predictions fail to materialize.

Puddleglum is equally pessimistic about the prospects for their journey. He does not see much chance of their finding their way north: They are traveling at the beginning of winter, through giant country, in search of a prince who probably isn't there, by way of a ruined city that no one has seen. He even throws in a little false optimism by saying that the bright side of things is that rough terrain, enemies, fatigue, and hunger will probably take their minds off the weather.

Finally, Eustace loses his temper. He has been badly frightened by talk of giants. He tells Puddleglum he does not believe their journey could be as hopeless as the Marshwiggle says it is. Otherwise, Aslan would not have sent them. He accuses Puddleglum of exaggerating the difficulties of their quest, just as he has the discomfort of his wigwam. Puddleglum sees in Eustace's tirade only an indication that their adventure is going sour even before they start. Puddleglum is not angry, but he cautions Eustace that it would be best to postpone the inevitable deterioration of their mutual relationship.

Puddleglum's negativism has a rather unpredictable effect on the children. You might expect him to demoralize them so that they will give up, defeated. This does not happen mainly because they almost immediately begin to discount practically everything pessimistic and cautionary that he says. In fact, they don't take him seriously enough at times. Jill is ready to blab their whole story about being sent by Aslan to find Prince Rilian when they meet the witch at the giant bridge, even though Puddleglum has warned her not to trust strangers. The results of that indiscretion could have been disastrous. Even after the witch is gone, Jill and Eustace are sure Puddleglum is wrong about her. Only painful experience teaches them differently.

There are times, however, when a negative word from Puddleglum really does dampen the children's spirits. When Jill falls into a trench in their struggle to cross what turns out to be the ruined city, she is discouraged from exploring farther by Puddleglum's warning that she might be walking into a dragon's cave or might encounter giant earthworms or beetles. Since she is already afraid of narrow places, this extra pessimism is too much for her, and she retreats. Usually, however, the dire words of their leader simply provide a rather comical backdrop to their travels.

Aside from his habits of speech, Puddleglum has some very valuable characteristics as a guide. He is experienced in wandering the wilderness. He shows Jill and Eustace how to stay warm by sleeping back to back and putting both blankets on top. He is good at shooting birds on the moor to sustain a rather meager existence. And he has a general idea of where they need to go and the dangers they will meet on the way. Since practically everyone they meet on their journey is either an enemy or dangerous, a cautious guide is a good thing to have around.

Even though Puddleglum is dead set against going to Harfang, Jill and Eustace overrule him and insist on heading in that direction. But he makes the best he can of what he considers to be a bad situation. He makes them promise not to divulge to the Gentle Giants either the fact that they began their journey in Narnia or the purpose of their expedition. Unknowingly, they are headed in the right direction, if only Jill had remembered the four signs Aslan gave her before he sent her into Narnia. They could have followed Aslan's instructions without getting into Harfang. But once they arrive at that awesome place, their promise to Puddleglum keeps them from a fatal disclosure, helps promote the image of absolute simplicity that they communicate to the giants, and eventually makes escape possible.

Puddleglum proves he is not being cowardly in not wanting to go to Harfang by what he does when they arrive. He says they must "put a bold face on it." So he charges right up to the front door and asks for lodging. Once inside, he is not a great deal of help. He begins by having too much of a drink offered him by the giants' porter and is incapacitated for the rest of the evening. Once he sobers up, Puddleglum is not capable of putting on the act of innocence and enthusiasm about the Autumn Feast that Jill does. In fact, if the giants had noticed his attempt to assume "a gay and gamesome attitude," it might have ruined everything. The Marshwiggle has many serious and sensible qualities, but acting is not one of them.

Puddleglum does keep the children from simply asking the giants' permission to leave Harfang, and he helps them make good their escape by advising Jill and Eustace not to run down the road from Harfang to the ruined city. When they are being pursued by the hounds, he finds a way under the city, where pursuit cannot follow.

It is not until the little party is underground that Puddleglum comes into his own. When they first meet the mournful-looking gnomes, Puddleglum rubs his hands with glee and says, "This is just what I needed. If these chaps don't teach me to take a serious view of life, I don't know what will." Despite the fact that Jill is afflicted with claustrophobia, Puddleglum calms her down enough to get her through a narrow place in which they must crawl on their faces for what seems like an hour. Lewis tells us that the children "had thought him a wet blanket while they were still above ground, but down here he seemed the only comforting thing they had."

When they meet the enchanted knight in the witch's dark castle, Puddleglum exposes a flaw in the knight's twisted logic. Jill and Eustace reveal that they have come to the underworld in obedience to Aslan's instructions and the words inscribed on the ruined city. The knight says the words "Under Me" are simply part of a longer verse composed by an ancient giant king. Puddleglum counters that Aslan knew that all of the words except the last two would wear away so that the three travelers would know what to do when they came to the city. The knight says in that case Aslan must be a "long liver." But Puddleglum responds that the witch must be a "long liver," too, to remember the original inscription on the city. Thus he keeps Jill and Eustace from losing their faith in Aslan at a crucial juncture.

Throughout the scene that follows, Puddleglum is a tower of strength. He keeps his wits about him, enabling the children to survive their difficult encounters with the witch and the knight, whom she has enchanted. When the knight invites them to come back while he is in the silver chair, Jill is reluctant to return. But Puddleglum says that they need all the information they can get. So they return, only to find that the enchanted knight with something wrong about his face is Prince Rilian of Narnia.

Puddleglum is a strange combination of positive and negative character traits, but the combination serves to make him all the more believable. Lewis is reputed to have modeled the Marshwiggle after his gardener, who helped him maintain his property for thirty-four years. The gardener, F. W. Paxford, is described as being "an inwardly optimistic, outwardly pessimistic, dear, frustrating, shrewd countryman of immense integrity."

The fact that Puddleglum is really optimistic, despite what he says, becomes clear by the end of the book. His pessimistic statements are a characteristic of the race of Marshwiggles. When he returns to Narnia, he doesn't even want to tell the Narnians his story. Instead, he wants to hear all the bad news. Everyone just laughs and says, "Isn't that just like a Marshwiggle?" But even the other Marshwiggles recognize that Puddleglum's pessimism is phony. They tell him, "You're altogether too full of bobance and bounce and high spirits. You've got to learn that life isn't all fricasseed frogs and eel pie." Jill summarizes the situation well when she kisses him good-bye. "'Puddleglum!' said Jill. 'You're a regular old humbug. You sound as doleful as a funeral and I believe you're perfectly happy. And you talk as if you were afraid of everything, when you're really as brave as—as a lion.'"

To all outward appearance Puddleglum is just like any other Marshwiggle living in the alluvial plain of the River Shribble, but he goes far beyond their limited outlook. If he really believed all of those gloomy sayings, he would give up, defeated, before they even left. But he acts courageously and steadfastly in accordance with his real character. He is not only a glum guide, but he is also a true friend and companion.

The Signs of the Times

The adventurers have been sent to seek the lost Prince Rilian and bring him back to his father's court. The guidance they receive on how to pursue their quest is symbolic of God's guidance in the Christian life. The signs Aslan gives Jill to guide them are symbolic of the place the Bible should have in the believer's life.

The four signs are: Eustace must greet an old friend as soon as he arrives in Narnia; they must seek the ruined city of the ancient giants; they must obey the message inscribed in the stones of that city; and the first person they meet in their travels who addresses them by the name of Aslan will be the true prince.

The signs are not general principles that are intended to shape the seekers' characters. They are specific instructions that are like signposts along the road through a strange country. The Bible likewise contains these two kinds of direction. The Ten Commandments and the Golden Rule are general rules that help men develop as moral creatures. These moral principles are essential for man to function in the least abrasive and most socially supportive way possible. They must be obeyed by all men. Not following them carries its own punishment. Perhaps, if a man were very clever and observant, he could figure them out for himself.

But man has not followed the moral code God has written into nature and his heart, and man needs a way to escape. God has provided the redemption story as the essential signpost of a way out of the dilemma. It is a signpost man could never have imagined. This and other signposts, such as the Holy Spirit's coming with power for the believer and daily guidance for personal problems, are the specific signs that lead the believer into the path God has prepared for him.

Jill thinks she has understood when the lion gives his instructions, but he tells her she has not understood as well as she thinks. So he patiently goes over the signs with Jill, until she can say them perfectly. Lewis is illustrating the need for Bible memorization. It is not sufficient to be acquainted with the truth, or even to be familiar with it. If it is to do any good in the rough and tumble of daily existence, it must be an integral part of the Christian.

Aslan reemphasizes this point as he is about to blow Jill to Narnia. Above all, she must remember the signs. He even advises a daily routine for rehearsing the signs and making sure she still knows them. She is to say them when she wakes up in the morning, when she goes to bed at night, and when she wakes in the middle of the night. The emphasis is on daily devotions. No matter how well the believer knows the Bible or how familiar he is with God's plan for his life, it will tend to slip away if he does not daily renew his acquaintance with God and His Word.

Aslan says that on the mountaintop, where the air is clear, it is easy to follow the signs. But when Jill drops into Narnia, the air will thicken:

"Take great care that it does not confuse your mind. And the Signs which you have learned here will not look at all as you expect them to look, when you meet them there. That is why it is so important to know them by heart and pay no attention to appearances. Remember the Signs and believe the Signs. Nothing else matters."

Many Christians' lives begin with mountaintop experiences; there is an emotional high that makes the new Christian feel very close to God. At this time it is easy to become engrossed in the Bible and to absorb its lessons. But later on it becomes harder. The believer descends to a more normal emotional plain, or even to a valley of discouragement. The air really is thicker down there, and it may seem far away from God and His Word.

Aslan warns Jill about appearances too. The believer may not always know who his friends are, and it may not always be easy to distinguish a right course of action from a disastrous one. The Prince Rilian rescue party receives several lessons in the deceptiveness of appearances.

The expedition begins badly. For several reasons, Eustace fails to obey the first sign and greet an old friend upon his arrival in Narnia: He was not around to hear Aslan's instructions; when Jill catches up with him, he is too angry with her for pushing him off the cliff to listen to what she has to say; and he does not recognize his old friend, King Caspian, because he has aged from a boy to an old man since Eustace saw him last. Aslan's warning has come true already. Caspian's altered appearance has kept Eustace from recognizing the king and obeying the first sign. If he had listened to Jill or heard Aslan's instructions himself, he could have discovered who the old man was. He suspects he is in Narnia, the old man who is departing is obviously the king, and he knows that Narnia time does not flow in sequence with our time. Putting all these facts together, he might have surmised the truth. But his anger keeps him from thinking about it hard enough.

Because they have muffed the first sign, Jill and Eustace must suffer the consequences. Trumpkin tells them that seeing an old friend would have brought Caspian's youth back for a moment. The owl tells them that more than thirty champions have disappeared in pursuit of Prince Rilian and that now no one is allowed to go. Jill and Eustace could probably have persuaded Caspian to let them go, and Caspian would have helped them—possibly with an army. But Trumpkin will allow no deviations from the rule in the king's absence. Therefore, they must sneak away from Cair Paravel at night.

Their initial setback discourages Jill and Eustace, but it does not stop them. Jill tells the owls that they have to be in earnest about their search for the lost prince, because she remembers Aslan's voice and face. She has met her master and is prepared to follow him, even if her path includes much stumbling. So, although they have missed the easiest means of following their quest, they proceed onward under the guidance of Puddleglum.

Having missed the first sign, the three wanderers must concentrate on the remaining three signs. So they set off in search of the ruined city of the ancient giants. Through a combination of good and bad motives, they manage to come to the ruined city. They start with the good intention of finding Prince Rilian by way of the ruined city, but after meeting the witch, Jill and Eustace are really looking for Harfang, which is just beyond their objective.

But visibility is poor in the driving snow, and they are so cold that they fail to recognize their objective once they reach it. They climb up the old stairs, struggle across the remains of old walls, see a five-hundred-foot section of wall that is still standing, and fall into one of the letters Aslan told them to look for. But only Puddleglum begins to realize the truth. The others are so eager to go on to Harfang that they will not listen to the Marsh-wiggle. When he asks Jill what the next sign is, she gets the order wrong, because she has neglected saying them every night, as Aslan instructed her to do.

Once again, failing to obey the signs has damaging consequences. They are caught in a giant trap, simply because they failed to stop to consider the evidence at the right moment. Aslan appears to Jill in a dream, and she finds she has forgotten all the signs. He carries her to the window and shows her the ruined city under the moonlight, and she sees the instruction of the third sign, UNDER ME. Because they have been disobedient by not discovering and obeying this command, they must plan a harrowing escape from the cannibalistic Gentle Giants. They even find themselves eating a talking stag before they make good their escape. In Puddleglum's mind, this is the equivalent of eating a baby. Although they don't know until it is too late that they are participating in the giants' cannibalism, Puddleglum rightly remarks that it would not have happened if they had obeyed the signs.

Once again, disobedience causes pain and suffering, but there is a difference between the events at the ruined city and their failure to greet King Caspian. Once the king is gone, it is too late to make amends, and they must go without the promised help. At the ruined city, they finally comply with Aslan's instructions, but their timing is wrong. As a result, they must endure the danger of being eaten, the memory of eating a soulish beast, and a pins-and-needles departure from the giants' castle. Even when they are running from Harfang to the ruined city, under hot pursuit, they have no idea how reaching it will help. But a way under opens up at the last moment.

There are two ways of doing the Lord's will: the hard way and the easy way. The hard way, initial disobedience to His will that is followed by eventual compliance, always seems easier in the beginning but invariably leads us to deadly precipices. It seems easier in the snow and cold to push on to Harfang than to stop for analysis of unusual surroundings. But a five-minute conference on the flat hill might have saved them two days in the jaws of the giants. It is difficult to learn that it is easier to do the Lord's will first, even though it appears harder than another way.

The adventurers have already muffed three signs. One sign was irrevocable. They had only one chance to obey and failed. The second and third signs were finally complied with, but only under hazardous circumstances. The travelers have only one more sign to aid them. Appearances for the fourth sign are just as deceptive as they were for the first three. Jill, Eustace, and Puddleglum meet a loud, boisterous knight who acts like a puppy dog in matters concerning his queen. There is something wrong about his face, and he has no feelings for the nation he is about to destroy. Moreover, he belittles Aslan and the second and third signs. All external indications are that he is not Prince Rilian.

But he wants company while he is tied to the silver chair, so he invites his guests to come back and join him during his midnight ravings. They do, but only after promising each other not to listen to and untie the knight. But the temporarily unenchanted prince calls to them, in the name of Aslan, to release him, and they are caught in a dilemma. They have no reason to believe he is the prince, but why have they learned the signs if they aren't going to obey them? Puddleglum recognizes immediately what they must do. They must obey the sign, regardless of what happens. He reminds the children that they have no guarantee that everything will be all right if they do so. In fact, he expects the opposite. But he feels it is their duty to obey the sign, even at the cost of their lives. So for once they go against appearances and obey their instructions, and everything does come right. The hard choice has become the easy choice.

Puddleglum is right. God does not guarantee good times or an easy path. But He does promise that, for the Christian, all things work together for good, though not necessarily to his convenience. And the Lord promises an inward satisfaction and joy to sustain the believer in his hour of need. The liberated prince has the right attitude. When he goes for his shield, he finds that it has turned from black to silver with a bright lion on it. "'Doubtless,' said the Prince, 'This signifies that Aslan will be our good lord, whether he means us to live or die. And all's one, for that.'" He repeats his theme when they are left in darkness in the witch's new diggings: "Whether we live or die Aslan will be our good lord." Prince Rilian's words echo those of the apostle Paul: "For to me to live is Christ, and to die is gain" (Phil. 1:21).

Poison Green and the Magnitude of Evil

The Narnia books give different perspectives on evil. In the previous books, evil has generally manifested itself in rather obvious ways; *The Silver Chair* gives a subtle and sophisticated picture of evil. As in *The Lion, the Witch and the Wardrobe*, a witch is the chief characterization of evil. But this witch is vying for control of Narnia and is not in command, as the White Witch was. Therefore, the Lady of the Green Kirtle hides her true nature when she is outside her underworld kingdom.

The witch begins her assault on Narnia by fatally poisoning the queen, while in her snake form. Then she does something even more damaging by enchanting the crown prince, Rilian. She shows herself to him as a beautiful woman, and he is totally enraptured by her appearance. The Lord Drinian recognizes her as wicked, but Prince Rilian is completely taken in. Even Jill and the owls think the green snake and the green lady are the same creature, but they were not under her spell at the time. It is easier to see another's blind spots than to see one's own. Jill proves the principle by subsequently falling under the witch's spell on the road to the ruined city. Jill and Eustace are ready to throw caution to the wind and tell everything to the enchanting lady with the thrilling voice and the gorgeous pony. What makes this even more remarkable is the fact that the witch is dressed in poison green, exactly as she was when she beckoned to Rilian in the Lord Drinian's presence. Rilian has the excuse that he saw the witch as a snake only before falling under her spell as a woman. But Jill and Eustace have the benefit of Drinian's vision. All of this melts away in the company of glittering evil.

Wickedness is known by its fruits, just as righteousness is, and the witch's wily words about Harfang bring forth a crop of discontentment, anger, forgetfulness, and extreme danger. Jill and Eustace spar with each other and with Puddleglum. They become impatient with skinny fowl and rocky beds and the cold wilderness. All they can think about is hot beds and baths at Harfang. The irony of the situation is that the thing they most long for is arriving at the Autumn Feast of the Gentle Giants, where the chief delicacy is to be themselves. All of this becomes clear as they stand by the window of the giants' castle and read Aslan's instructions inscribed on the stones of the ruined city, and as they read in the giants' cookbook how the delicate biped man is to be prepared. But the witch has accomplished her purpose of distracting her pursuers by sending them to her colleagues in crime, the giants.

The civilized giants of Harfang are an interesting study in themselves. They are not quite as clever as the witch is, but they have no trouble in fooling two children and one Marshwiggle. They even appear to be mannerly, hospitable, sympathetic, and very kind to their little guests. The giants provide their visitors with all the food and drink they want, as well as the promised hot baths and beds. Some of the giantesses even seem sorry, in a hypocritical sort of way, that they will soon be eating their cute little guests. Although they do not lack civilization, the giants have little virtue.

Eventually certain things come out that give the wanderers a clue to what their hosts really have in mind for them. The giant king licking his lips with his large, red tongue is a little disconcerting. The fact that everyone laughs when they say they have come for the Autumn Feast is somewhat stranger. Discovering that the giants eat talking animals jars with the civilized trappings of Harfang. Finally, the recipes for man and Marshwiggle make the witch's intentions unmistakably clear to them. They have been had.

Civilization by itself is no substitute for righteousness. Some of the world's most advanced nations have caused some of the most horrible carnage. Some of the most congenial and intellectual people around have espoused some of the most wrongheaded, perverted, and destructive philosophies.

Once Jill, Eustace, and Puddleglum obey Aslan's sign and go underground, they find out what the witch is like in her own realm. Her servants, the gnomes of Bism, are zombies. They are incredibly varied, but all are sad. They are a nation of sleepwalkers. In the witch's capital city, the gnomes are as busy and silent as they are sad. Evil is a hard taskmaster. It drives a man all day, troubles his sleep all night, robs him of true joy and laughter, and makes him forget how really to have fun.

The enchanted prince portrays another manifestation of evil. He laughs, but too loudly. One of the things he laughs about is the humor of his sudden destruction of an unsuspecting nation. There is something wrong with his face. His past has been taken away from him. He is the lackey of a woman whose virtues he affirms without being able to support. Lewis likens his appearance to that of Hamlet. And indeed his position resembles that of the troubled prince of Denmark. Hamlet wants to avenge the treacherous death of his father, but his doing so is delayed by inward doubts and the fact that his mother is implicated in the treachery. Prince Rilian sets out to avenge the death of his mother but becomes infatuated by his mother's destroyer. He is bound to inactivity by the witch's enchantment, which is manifested by the silver chair.

The silver chair is a symbol that ostensibly represents royalty and wealth and is even purported to have a therapeutic value on the deluded prince. Actually it stands for bondage and slavery. Chains forged from gold or silver are just as confining as those made of iron. The knight fancies himself as the future king of a captured country, but his real destiny would have been that of the puppet of a wicked witch. The Christian must beware compromising his beliefs in trade for such a gilded cage.

The real impact of the witch on those she controls becomes clear when the liberated gnome captured by Puddleglum tells his story. She had wiped out all remembrance of fun and dancing and laughter and the dazzling country of Bism. A wise dwarf summarizes the situation at the end of the book. He says, "Those Northern Witches always mean the same thing, but in every age they have a different plan for getting it." In every age Satan has a different plan for enslaving man. He might use mystery religions, as he did at the time of Christ. Or he might use the Inquisition, as he did during the Middle Ages. Or he might rely on witchcraft, as he did in Elizabethan England. Or he might turn to dictators like Hitler and Mussolini. But his intention is always the same. He means to trick, betray, bind, and kill mankind.

Archetype and Ectype

The various threads of meaning that run through *The Silver Chair* come together nicely in the climactic scene far underground in the witch's castle, where the witch meets Rilian, Jill, Eustace, and Puddleglum. Prince Rilian has just been freed from his enchantment and has destroyed the symbol of the witch's power over him: the silver chair. Rilian thinks he is free, but he has yet to prove he can resist the wooing of the witch. She is very angry to see her designs frustrated, but she is smart enough to know the battle is not yet lost.

The witch begins by weighing the odds in her favor. She uses the drugging smell of a green powder and the hypnotic effect of a monotonous strumming on a mandolin to dull the senses and minds of her hearers. Then she sows despair in their hearts by pretending that there is no other world than the dismal confines of her underground kingdom. She does not directly attack her victims for believing in Narnia and the world aboveground; she just laughs at them and pretends they are playing a game of make-believe.

After setting the mood, adopting her sweetest manner, and consciously trying to gain control of her listeners' minds and emotions, she specifically attacks their memories outside of her dark kingdom. First, she indicates that Narnia is a pretend world that they have all made up or dreamed of. The witch jumps on Jill's assertion that she comes from still another world and asks her what chariots go between their worlds. Of course, Jill cannot explain this. Then Puddleglum alludes to the brightest feature of the Narnian world: their sun. When she asks Puddleglum to describe it, Prince Rilian interjects by comparing the sun to the lamp hanging from the ceiling. This gives the witch the opportunity to say that he has simply looked at the lamp, imagined a bigger and better lamp, and called it the sun. The witch takes the same tack when Jill says they were sent by Aslan, the great lion. When pressed to describe a lion, Eustace says they are a little like very large cats. The witch accuses him of extrapolating from cats and imagining lions. Finally, everyone except Puddleglum gives in to the soft despair of the witch.

The witch is successful because she capitalizes on the tyranny of the now. That which is immediate seems much more possible than anything from the past or something at a distance. The children begin to believe they have been wrong and that they could have made it up. They do not realize that language is based on their senses, and their words have described physical realities.

The fact that man must speak with words derived from his physical surroundings should not limit the believer's apprehension of things and ideas and persons beyond his immediate physical purview. When Satan says that human fathers are the archetype and that God is the ectype, he has the order reversed. Actually, God is the archetype, and human fathers are the ectypes created by God and modeled after Him. God has created man in His own image. The Christian's God is not anthropomorphic; rather, man is theomorphic, created by God, in His image, and for His glory. Of course, there are similarities between God and man. For this reason, Satan should not be allowed to take a condition that supports man's divine origin and turn it into an argument against God's existence and power. Lewis cogently explains this concept in his first Christian book, *The Pilgrim's Regress*.

Puddleglum uses exactly the right reaction to the witch's conjuration. He recognizes that he cannot think clearly until the smell that is drugging them is reduced; so, despite the pain it causes his foot, he walks over and stamps on the fire. Lewis remarks that pain is the best curative for certain kinds of magic.

Once Puddleglum's mind is clear, he tells the witch exactly what he thinks. Being the pessimistic creature he is, he does not question the truth of what the witch is saying. Being confined to a world without grass or sky or sun or stars or Aslan is just what this glum guide would expect to encounter. But he says that if he and Jill and Eustace and Rilian have made up a world with all those wonderful things, then their imaginings are far better than the real world of the witch's dark pit. It is unlikely that the glorious world of Narnia could have been imagined based on experiences in a hole. Moreover, if the witch's world is all there is, there is no point in living. If they do not wish to despair and die, they may as well go on the assumption that Narnia exists and die searching for it.

Puddleglum's words apply to the searching non-Christian as well. Only a life in Christ offers the fulfillment and meaning a person needs. If He does not exist, then life is a hopeless fraud. Every plan and scheme will come to nothing, and man may as well give up without a struggle. But if there is even a chance that the Bible is true and Christ has died to obliterate sins and make men children of God, surely that chance is worth pursuing. Only Jesus can open a way into the black pit that engulfs mankind and from which there is no exit. Without His help, we are already entombed.

The Other Side

The Silver Chair ends as it began, with a visit to Aslan's country. Aslan appears to Jill and Eustace in Narnia to take them back to Experiment House via his peaceable kingdom. Jill instantly recalls all of her failures and is downcast, but Aslan is not harsh with her. One could do much worse than to be greeted in heaven with the message that Aslan gives Jill and Eustace: "Think of that no more. I will not always be scolding. You have done the work for which I sent you into Narnia." This is not quite Jesus' "Well done, good and faithful servant," but it is not too far removed from that hoped-for greeting.

Aslan takes them to his country because he wants to show them the other side of death and because he wants to correct even seemingly small problems like Experiment House. When they arrive on Aslan's mountain, they still hear funeral music and see the dead king. Everyone weeps for him, even Aslan. It is like Jesus weeping for Lazarus just before He raised him from the dead. Aslan commands Eustace to prick his paw with a sharp thorn, which produces a large drop of blood. That drop falls into the stream where Caspian's corpse lies and brings him back to an ageless life.

This is another reference to Christ's atoning blood shed for mankind. Sinful man requires a perfect sacrifice to rescue him from the deadly consequences of his sin. Christians can trace their eternal existence in God's presence to the prints in Jesus' hands as surely as Caspian traces his revivification to the mark of the thorn in Aslan's paw.

This whole section of *The Silver Chair* is reminiscent of 1 Thessalonians 4:13–18. The apostle Paul recognizes that people will miss those who pass on before them, just as Jill and Eustace sorrow for Caspian. Even Jesus wept at the sight of suffering and death, though He was on the verge of reversing it. But believers do not sorrow as do those who have no hope. Although the Christian can now see only this side of his loved ones' passing, let him remember that the other side, the reawakening in heaven, occurs only moments after the leave-taking. The contrast between the decrepit and dying king and the joyously rejuvenated boy-man shows how jubilant is that awakening for those who cross over.

7

The Last Battle

The final book in Lewis's series tells of the end of the world of Narnia. Like the earth, Narnia cannot last forever, and life there is only a reflection of eternal life with Aslan. Combining the truth he had written in *The World's Last Night* and Jesus' account, in Matthew 24, of the end of the world, Lewis's description of the Narnian last days is brilliant in its conception, dazzling in its execution, achingly beautiful, unspeakably sad, and gloriously hopeful.

The Great Deceit

The Last Battle begins with a great lie created by a wizened old ape named Shift, who has a wrong sense of his own self-importance and self-interest. He is as clever as he is ugly, and he concocts a way of putting the whole nation of Narnia under his feet. He has already made overtures to the Tisroc of Calormen, who would love to add Narnia to his extensive empire. The Calormenes eventually become too much for Shift, but in the beginning, he fancies himself as controlling the destiny of nations. The ape's name is significant, as are many names in this book. He shifts his allegiance from Narnia to Calormen; from Aslan to Tashlan to Tash; from his friend Puzzle the Donkey to the treacherous Rishda Tarkaan.

An old lion's skin floating in Caldron Pool gives the vicious Shift a chance to put his schemes into action. After conning Puzzle into fishing the skin out of the pool, Shift's mind begins to work. He sees in this small incident an opportunity to gain power over the talking creatures of Narnia. He puts the lion's skin on Puzzle and does his best to make the donkey look like a lion. The end product is not too convincing, but Shift plans to show Puzzle at night, from a distance, and in poor light, to creatures who have never seen a lion. Shift rightly concludes that it will work.

The only problem is getting Puzzle to go along. The donkey is rather slow mentally, but he is good-hearted. He does not want to pretend to be Aslan, even though Shift tells him he can get the creatures to do whatever he wants. Puzzle does not care about power, but Shift argues that Puzzle could do a lot of good for Narnia, acting under Shift's advice. Shift even claims that Aslan sent the skin on purpose so that Puzzle could wear it. When Puzzle asks what would happen if Aslan showed up, Shift argues that he never does show up these days.

Then a thunderclap and an earthquake hurl them both to the ground. Aslan is warning both Shift and Puzzle that they are in grave danger of offending him, but Shift cleverly claims the signs should be taken the opposite way. He states he was about to say that those signs should be given if they are to proceed with the plan.

Within the first pages of *The Last Battle*, these words of Christ are already being echoed:

> See to it that no one misleads you. For many will come in My name, saying, "I am the Christ," and will mislead many.... Then if anyone says to you, "Behold, here is the Christ," or "There He is," do not believe him. For false Christs and false prophets will arise and will show great signs and wonders, so as to mislead, if possible, even the elect. Behold, I have told you in advance. So if they say to you, "Behold, He is in the wilderness," do not go out, or "Behold, He is in the inner rooms," do not believe them. For just as the lightning comes from the east and flashes even to the west, so will the coming of the Son of Man be.
>
> Matthew 24:4–5, 23–27 NASB

Shift intends to mislead the Narnians into thinking that Aslan has returned. He plans to show them a false Aslan, who is really a donkey dressed up in a lion's skin. He means to enlist them as slaves to the false Aslan. He is, in fact, a false prophet pointing to a false lord who is actually dependent on himself. Shift is a little short on great wonders, other than his nightly presentation of

Puzzle, but he makes up for it in pretended wonders, such as the supposed devouring of King Tirian by the false Aslan. The "wilderness" referred to in Matthew 24 becomes Lantern Waste in Narnia, and the "inner rooms" become a simple stable. These elements form the framework for the great deceit that Shift perpetrates on the land of Narnia.

Even Christ's words about misleading the elect are portrayed. Puzzle defers to the wisdom of his false friend Shift, even to the point of consenting to become a false god. Yet Puzzle is a lover of the true Aslan, and he eventually escapes from his folly. The talking animals are too trusting to believe that someone would lie about such a thing, so they accept Shift's imitation as the real thing. Even King Tirian and Jewel are initially taken in. Jewel is a little skeptical, but only because it all seems too good to be true.

King Tirian does not begin to suspect the truth until Roonwit the Centaur tells him that the stars foretell some great calamity, not the coming of Aslan. This passage seems to smack a bit of astrology, but the stars in Narnia are people, not gaseous objects. Lewis is not advocating the use of astrology in this world. If he had been writing in today's environment of widespread belief in and popularization of the occult, perhaps he would have written this passage differently. At any rate, Jesus tells us there will be signs of His coming and of the end of the age. The stars provide one of those signs in Narnia.

A more cogent sign, however, is what the false Aslan is actually doing. The king finds out that soulish Narnian trees are being killed, and he flies into a rage. He determines he will get to the bottom of the situation at once. In response to Roonwit's message and to the death of the dryads, Jewel miserably responds, in what is to become one of the book's watchwords, that Aslan is not a tame lion. Shift will use this theme to justify any kind of unlawful action. God *has* made the laws and given them to man, but His laws correspond with His character; He will violate neither His own character nor the laws that reflect that character, although some principles take precedence over others.

Tirian has already begun to guess the new Aslan is a fake before he sees Aslan's mouthpiece, "Lord Shift." Shift is dressed up in such a ridiculous fashion that he would be humorous, if he weren't so malicious. Wearing an ill-fitting scarlet jacket, jeweled slippers that won't stay on, and a paper crown, and busily gnawing away at a great pile of nuts, he is a perfect picture of a petty tyrant. As he gives orders to the squirrels to bring more nuts, it is clear that the whole scheme is intended to glorify Shift, not Aslan. A true servant of God does not make much of himself—he makes much of the God he serves. True devotion brings humility, not pride. Pride may sneak in unawares, when one of God's children is made much of; but if his devotion is deep enough, he will keep coming back to the realization that it is the Lord who builds His house. His children may help under His guidance, but it is God who gives the increase. Self-sacrifice, not selfishness, is the mark of a true Christian.

Another clue to Shift's fakery comes when he tells the animals that Aslan will no longer speak to them directly. He denies that Aslan used to do so in the old days, and he claims that only he, Shift, is worthy of addressing Aslan. Then he repeats the by-now-familiar refrain that Aslan is not a tame lion. Shift's contention directly contradicts the truth of the apostle Paul's statement in 1 Timothy 2:5 (NASB), "For there is one God, and one mediator also between God and men, the man Christ Jesus."

Shift gives a third hint of unholiness at the stable, when he lies about his origin and claims to be a man rather than an ape. Anyone with eyes can see that this hairy creature is an ape, but the Narnians have been cowed by Shift's pronouncements. When a Christian catches a supposed prophet in a lie, even in something trivial, he should steer clear of him. God is a God of truth and cannot tolerate dishonesty. But, as the Bible tells us, the devil was a liar from the beginning. He started lying to man and woman in the Garden of Eden, and he hasn't stopped since.

A fourth indication of the unholy origin of Shift's scheme is his plans for the talking animals. He intends to sell them into slavery to the Tisroc. He tries to cover this up by saying that they will be paid wages, which, however, will be diverted to the Narnian treasury in an arrangement that reminds us of Communism. He even goes so far as to say that the money thus earned will be used to bring all sorts of improvements to Narnia. There will be oranges and bananas (which Shift alone craves), "... roads and big cities and schools and offices ..." (which are totally useless in a country of talking animals), and "... whips and muzzles and saddles and cages and kennels and prisons ..." (symbols of slavery and oppression).

Once again, Lewis is showing the truth of the biblical dictum "you will know them by their fruits." Jesus came that men might have life and have it more abundantly. He does not promise an easy life, but He does promise an abundant one. Wherever the Gospel has been fully accepted, freedom and social justice have followed. Before Shift's takeover Narnia was a good example of how that freedom can operate.

The final and overwhelming clue to Shift's despicability comes when he claims that Aslan and Tash, the Calormene god, are one. He even mixes the names into a hybrid: Tashlan. He has become a liberal theologian. Shift tells the animals that they have been narrow-minded in supposing themselves right and the Calormenes wrong. Really, Aslan and Tash are just two words for the same being. Clearly, this passage is designed to contradict those who would have us believe that the word *God* is big enough to encompass all religions—those who claim that it doesn't much matter what you believe, so long as you are sincere. Lewis believed in the validity of propositional truth and the rationality of the universe. He did not have much patience with those who play around with concepts like paradoxical logic to replace old-fashioned Aristotelian logic. People who deny the truth may make themselves blind to it, but they do not obliterate its existence. Shift and Rishda Tarkaan and Ginger the Cat are all blind to the reality of both Aslan and Tash, God and Satan, but they learn ultimately that they have made a terrible mistake in denying divine and satanic reality.

Another characteristic of the big lie becomes clear when King Tirian tries to speak out against the ape. He is immediately clobbered and silenced. Darkness cannot tolerate light or abide with it, so it tries to keep the light hidden. Persecution is always a characteristic of religious error, and even a country's king may not be immune from it. But Tirian learns a valuable lesson through his ordeal. He knows now that Shift is a cheat, because he claims that Tash and Aslan are one. Tirian recognizes this as nonsense and feels much better about the fact that it is Shift and not Aslan who is raping Narnia.

The stable in which Puzzle has been staying represents a false appearance of Aslan, as opposed to the true incarnation of Christ in Bethlehem. All the Narnians come to the stable to worship their lord, just as the shepherds and wise men came to adore Jesus. But the Narnians are gloom-filled at Puzzle's appearance, unlike the shepherds and wise men. Lucy makes one of the few direct statements connecting Narnia with Christianity when she compares Puzzle's stable with the one in which Christ was born.

Courage and perseverance are the key ingredients in exposing falsehood, and Jill displays them both in rescuing Puzzle from the stable. She threatens him with her knife, but he is quite willing to come. He is beginning to see how wrong he has been in going along with Shift and how he has been mistreated in the bargain.

Once they have Puzzle, Tirian and his party think they can expose him as the fake Aslan. Their optimism quickly fades, however, when they free a troop of dwarfs. The dwarfs move from belief in, or at least acceptance of, the false Aslan to a skepticism in the existence of any Aslan or the authority of any king. Lewis summarizes the situation well when he says, "Tirian had never dreamed that one of the results of an Ape's setting up a false Aslan would be to stop people from believing in the real one." That is often the case in this world as well, and Satan knows that a fake Christian is an even more powerful tool in his hands than a strong atheist. It is always the devil's intention to convince men that the Christian's gospel is hopeless and outmoded, and the effect of one false practitioner in achieving this goal is often greater than the influence of outright skeptics.

Eventually sin takes its toll, and even the gussied-up ape must move aside for others. He has put himself in contact with forces stronger than he is, and they finally assert their control over him. The ape knows that his influence is waning and starts drinking. Ginger and Rishda are now the prime planners, and the ape becomes their mouthpiece. They kick him and abuse him as they lead him onto center stage, and they let him live only because the talking animals look up to him.

Satan is no respecter of persons. He takes no better care of those who are loyal to him than anyone else. He will retain them as tools as long as they are useful, but he will cast them aside when their usefulness is ended.

Satan is eager to utilize honest and dedicated people, too. When Jewel is captured, he is persecuted and threatened with death unless he lies to the crowd about Puzzle. He stands fast and is finally rescued. If he had capitulated to his captors' demands, his reward for lying would have been the opportunity of having his horn sawed off and being sent to Calormen to draw a cart.

Puzzle's disappearance presents a problem to the renegade ape, but his friends help him solve it. Shift says that the real Aslan is still in the stable, but that a false one in a lion's skin is skulking about the woods. The beasts are enraged by this news and say that they will tear the false Aslan apart if they see him. What's more, the real Aslan is so mad about it, he will no longer come out of the stable. A little truth has made the ape's lie much stronger. There is now no point in showing Puzzle to the crowd, since Shift has already said he was a fake. Any truth that Tirian can offer can be contradicted by one of Shift's lies.

The ape's plot finally comes down to a great witch hunt. Shift tries to send all of his opponents forcibly through the stable door, supposedly to meet Tashlan, but actually to be slaughtered by a Calormene confederate. It is appropriate that the ape meets his end by being cast through the door to meet his real master, Tash, who devours him in one bite. He who lives by the sword shall die by the sword. And he who serves Satan can only look forward to one day being demolished by Satan. Eustace is correct when he says that it serves Shift right. Justice does, in the end, prevail. Shift fancied himself as being smarter than everyone else and concocted a scheme for capitalizing on their gullibility. But Shift finally becomes the victim of his own deceit. In blinding himself to the reality of Aslan, he has also deceived himself into thinking there is no Tash. He has cut himself off from Aslan's protection and becomes fair game for Tash's claws. Those who deny the existence of God and Satan should take note. Disbelieving in them will not keep them from one's doorstep.

Humility and Servility

Puzzle is a good donkey. His friend Shift is only a useless old ape who gives him no end of trouble, yet Puzzle is very loyal to the ape and does as well as he can to make the best of their relationship. Puzzle is also very diligent. Shift keeps his friend busy carrying water, shopping for delicacies only an ape could love, and generally serving Shift in any way that strikes his fancy. Puzzle is very humble; he knows that his mental capacity is very limited, so he lets Shift direct their actions. The donkey is in no danger of going off on a mental tangent of his own creation. He knows that other creatures are better suited for that sort of thing.

The problem is that Puzzle's laudable humility becomes a dangerous vice in the hands of Shift. Shift knows how to manipulate Puzzle to get him to do absolutely anything, including jumping into a treacherous, freezing pool after a worthless lion's skin. Puzzle does these things partly because he is afraid of losing his only friend, but mainly because he really cares about Shift and considers him brilliant. If Puzzle had picked a virtuous friend, all would have been well. But he becomes attached to Shift and does not seem to perceive the ape's viciousness.

The whole situation is still rather harmless, until the fatal lion's skin appears. Humble and slow as he is, Puzzle still knows it is wrong to pretend to look like Aslan. Regardless of the good he could do for others if they accepted him as a great authority, it is still wrong to pretend to be God. Puzzle knows this, but he is too softhearted to resist Shift's pouting when Puzzle does not want to put on the lion's skin. Once the skin is on, it is no easy matter to get it off again. When Shift tells the donkey all the good he could do for Narnia if he pretends to be Aslan, Puzzle is unimpressed. However, Puzzle weakens momentarily when Shift tells him there could be more sugar in Narnia. This is not enough, by itself, to change Puzzle's mind, but it does get him thinking. When the earthquake and thunderclap hit, Puzzle's good sense tells him he had better resist Shift's efforts to lead him astray, but he succumbs once more to Shift's quick thinking. Even Puzzle must see that Shift's explanation is not a plausible one, but perhaps the mention of sugar was just enough to convince him to do something that is even worse than he knows.

Puzzle has turned humility into servility by completely putting himself under the control of Shift, to the detriment of his own good judgment and prudence. He is surrendering himself to another created being, not Aslan. It takes a while for the enormity of his error to sink in to Puzzle. He is apologetic enough, but he keeps complaining that he thought the ape would know the right thing to do. He also points out that it was no picnic for him, being shut up in the stable in an uncomfortable skin, especially since his compatriots often forgot to bring him water. He seems to be saying that it is not so much he who has sinned as it is his friend Shift. Unfortunately, the analogy does not hold; he cannot get rid of his moral responsibility.

It is not until Puzzle sees the demon god Tash that he finally understands what he has done. The donkey's deception has brought the devil himself into their midst. Puzzle's confession of this is greeted by a rather unkind remark by Eustace that nonetheless summarizes the situation: "If you'd spent less time saying you weren't clever and more time trying to be as clever as you could. . . ." Having realized the truth of this, Puzzle is very apprehensive about meeting Aslan. He knows he has done wrong and would just as soon eat grass off by himself in paradise as meet the great lion. Lucy tells him it will be all right when Puzzle does meet him, and it is. Lewis does not reveal what Aslan tells Puzzle, but his first words make the donkey's ears droop and his next words make them perk up. Puzzle is sorry for what he has done, and while Aslan makes him aware of it, he does not belabor the issue.

The Sin of Despair

One of the most deadly weapons in Satan's entire arsenal is the sin of despair. Nothing can match its numbing, paralyzing capacity. It can take the most creative individual and turn him into a bore. It can stop a courageous struggler and force him into a retreat of seclusion. It can make the virtuous person striving to do right give up the fight. The devil can temporarily win the victory in believers' lives if he can chip away at the hope the Bible has given them.

An undercurrent of despair runs through *The Last Battle*. It begins early in the story and doesn't end until the heroes and heroines pass through the stable door into Aslan's country.

King Tirian's position is an unenviable one: He has inherited a beautiful kingdom with pleasant subjects, but he stands at the end of his world, watching the kingdom crumble away beneath him. With almost no warning of the impending doom, he is faced with the destruction of his kingdom and the murder of his subjects. One minute he is being warned by Roonwit the Centaur of a coming disaster, and the next, he learns of the killing of the dryads.

The king's initial reaction is rage. Although Roonwit counsels caution, he sets off with Jewel the Unicorn to have satisfaction from the interlopers who are dismembering Narnia. When he encounters two Calormenes abusing a talking horse, his will becomes divorced from reason, and he and Jewel strike down the Calormenes without warning.

When they have done the deed, they fall into despair. They have been told that Aslan is behind the killings. They can't comprehend why Aslan would needlessly kill his creatures, yet they cannot deny that he is not a tame lion. They feel, however, that Aslan may have changed his character; he is no longer the kind, wise, and just ruler they have always heard about. He seems to be capable of meaningless cruelty. They do not challenge him on this score, but wish to withdraw from the problem and let others witness the devastation of the land. When it seems Aslan is behind it, Tirian says, "If we had died before to-day we should have been happy." And Jewel responds, "We have lived too long. The worst thing in the world has come upon us." Their mood deepens when they murder the two Calormenes. Tirian summarizes the situation when he asks, "Would it not be better to be dead than to have this horrible fear that Aslan has come and is not like the Aslan we have believed in and longed for? It is as if the sun rose one day and were a black sun." Jewel adds that it is like drinking dry water, if Aslan is not Aslan.

In this mood of despair they both decide to turn themselves over to the Calormenes, because Tirian has not acted up to his kingly code of protection for all men, and Jewel will not let him go alone to the enemy. In acting in anger and despair, Tirian has lost his chance to protect Narnia. Because he has the allegiance of his people, he is in the best position to fight the Calormenes, but because of his despair he is unable to regain the position he has lost. His best efforts would not have saved his kingdom, but he could have mounted a better defense, had he not acted rashly.

Jewel and Tirian have not really exercised their faith in this incident. A cloud has been cast over their image of Aslan, and they sink down under it. Tirian's surrender to the Calormenes is as much a yielding to seemingly inevitable circumstances as it is the remorseful action of a dishonored knight. As king of Narnia, he owes it to his subjects to disclose his murder to them and listen to their advice before he gives himself up to an alien. By giving them no warning, he has left Narnia leaderless and at the mercy of Calormen. In consulting with his subjects, he would have given them fair warning to provide for a substitute leader who could mobilize and protect them.

The despairing gloom that envelops Tirian and Jewel has captured the other talking animals as well. They all groan and whimper when they see who has been taken prisoner. They grow sadder and sadder as Shift, in the name of the false Aslan, imposes more and more unreasonable and selfish demands on them. The crowning blow comes with the confusion of Tash and Aslan. Even when this absurdity is proclaimed, they do not object; they just mope. Their faces grow unspeakably sad, their tails hang down very straight, and their whiskers droop. Although Tirian tries to cheer them by giving the lie to Shift, they do not respond. They are even afraid of freeing or helping their bound king. Some of the smaller and bolder ones come in the dead of night to feed him, but they are too frightened of the fake Aslan to free Tirian. They still feel affection for their king, but not for the terrible Aslan they serve. They no longer want Aslan to be with them; they are now serving out of a fear of power rather than out of love and respect.

The Narnians are even less inquisitive than their king has been. Instead of realizing that not everyone who names the name of Aslan is his servant, they blindly accept Shift's midnight apparition and let the deadness grow within them. God's people are susceptible to the same malaise. When the concept of sin and Christ and salvation are challenged as being untrue, how do believers respond? Too often men shrink inside themselves and consider themselves virtuous for hanging on, with their last ounce of strength, to the faith. Like Tirian and Jewel, they are afraid that too much knowledge may destroy them. It seems as if too close an inquiry into an issue such as the infallibility of the Bible might destroy a man's faith. Yet if Christianity is true—and it is—man may scrutinize as closely as he likes. The end result will be to strengthen, not weaken, faith, because the Christian will find more evidence to support it.

The thing that jolts the king out of the worst of his depression is his realization that Shift must be selling a false Aslan with his claim that Tash and Aslan are one. Once he is sure that Aslan has not changed his character and become evil, Tirian still feels unlucky, but he no longer is mired in a deadly malaise. He remembers all the previous occasions when Narnia was in its direst straits and discovers that Aslan and children from another world always provided assistance in those troubled times. So he asks Aslan either to come himself or to send the children from another world, even though he has a feeling that things like that don't happen anymore. When he calls for the children, it is almost as if another were speaking through him, and he immediately appears as a ghost in this world at a dinner for the seven friends of Narnia. But his vision of the seven friends fades before he can speak to them. Lewis says waking from this dream was the worst moment in Tirian's life, because he has been close to help without being able to grab hold of it. His sorrow is broken, however, by the arrival of Jill and Eustace. He looks on them with wonder and thinks that anything might happen now.

The talking animals, to their detriment, do not follow the path pursued by their king. They have seen Aslan, and he is evil, but they are afraid of him and continue to bow down before him. Gloom and fear dominate Narnia. This is the woeful situation that Tirian tries to change. He starts with a company of dwarfs and succeeds in freeing them, but he cannot unlock their minds. Their thoughts have been poisoned by Ginger the Cat, and they no longer care for Aslan or kings or anyone but themselves. So they jeer at Tirian and go their own way.

This cools Tirian off a bit, and he begins to understand how difficult it will be to enlighten the deluded Narnian creatures. Poggin, the one dwarf who joins his side, informs him that Ginger has told the animals that Aslan has swallowed up Tirian, and they have become even more afraid. When Shift tells them at the last midnight meeting that a donkey is masquerading as Aslan and that the real Aslan is so mad he will no longer come out of the stable, the beasts are abject in anguish. The final straw in breaking their wills and shackling their minds occurs when Ginger goes into the stable to meet Tashlan and then streaks out in utter terror and loses the ability to speak. The worst thing that can happen to a talking beast is losing its speech, and Shift now has them in the palm of his hand. They want him always to intervene between Tashlan and them and to hide them from the horrible lion.

Even when Tirian jumps out of hiding and calls all loyal Narnians to himself, few respond. The dogs, some small creatures, the bear, and the boar join him. A few join the Calormene side. But most just sneak away or watch the unfolding spectacle. The majority of the talking animals are like the people described in Revelation 6:16, who will call on the rocks and mountains to fall on them and hide them from the wrath of God. They will not admit the error of their ways and repent. The talking animals know there is power inside the stable, and they worship that. When Tirian feeds Shift to Tash and the earth shakes, they fall on their faces and beg for protection. They have a fatal fascination with a power that both terrifies and mesmerizes them; what they fail to see is that their only escape is to join the side that is opposed to Tash and aligned with the real Aslan.

The Adventure Aslan Sends

There is a phrase that sparkles from the pages of *The Last Battle* like a small but perfect diamond. The first time King Tirian uses it, he doesn't quite get it right. When he and Jewel have seen the murder of the talking trees, Tirian tells Jewel that they must take the adventure that comes to them. Later, after Tirian calls for help from Aslan, and the children Jill and Eustace come, he starts saying it more correctly. He tells his visitors that he was not robbed of the keys to his guard tower "by Aslan's good will." The king is beginning to realize that events are not coming at him willy-nilly, with no reason. Aslan is allowing them to happen through his permissive will. The seven friends of Narnia realize the same thing when they try to manipulate their way into Narnia by using magic rings. They never get a chance to use the rings, because Aslan sends Jill and Eustace to Narnia, and the others to heaven via a train crash. It is obvious that Aslan prefers to be asked for his will rather than have his subjects force their wills on him.

Finally, at the end of all things, the phrase comes forth in full flower. When Farsight the Eagle tells King Tirian's party that Cair Paravel is in the hands of the Calormenes, that the Narnians are in rout, and that Roonwit is dead, Jewel stomps his foot and proclaims their destiny: "Nothing now remains for us seven but to go back to Stable Hill, proclaim the truth, and take the adventure that Aslan sends us." We meet the phrase again when Tirian tells Jill and Eustace they may accompany him and take "the adventure that Aslan would send them."

There are several more variations of the same thrilling theme, once in the touching scene where Jewel says goodbye to Tirian: "If Aslan gave me my choice I would choose no other life than the life I have had and no other death than the one we go to." Again, when Jill asks Tirian if Tash is inside the stable, he answers, "We are all between the paws of the true Aslan." Finally, before their last skirmish, as the king's party realizes that they will probably all pass through the stable door, Jewel tells them, "It may be for us the door to Aslan's country and we shall sup at his table tonight."

What are these creatures trying to say? Simply and profoundly, they are saying with their lives that God's way is best. There is no such thing as luck. He knows what is in store for the believer and is allowing it to happen. The Christian must be willing to place complete trust in Him.

The Cancer of Cunning

While common sense and shrewdness may be helpful to anyone, they can be overused to the point where the person becomes mentally and spiritually deprived. The prime examples of beings who suffer from this problem in this book are a group of troublesome little dwarfs. Led by a sneering chap named Griffle, they have been taken in, like everyone else, by Shift's fake Aslan. When Tirian shows them the donkey that has deceived them and frees them from the Calormenes, the dwarfs show no gratitude. Some of them have been let into the secret anyway and have only been going along with the deception in hope of gaining favor with the Tisroc. Once freed, they feel they owe allegiance to no one except themselves. "The Dwarfs are for the Dwarfs." Since they have seen one fake Aslan, they will not believe there is a real one, and their deception on that score makes them determined not to be deceived on any others: They will not believe Tirian is king, since he, too, may be a cheat; they will not accept Jill's story of another world, because they have never seen it. They will, in short, believe in nothing but what they can conclusively prove to themselves, and they will do nothing that is not in their own self-interest. And they will not believe that anyone else is motivated by anything other than the same selfishness. So they tell Tirian he has rescued them in order to use them in some game of his own. They think he wants to trick them just like "the other lot."

The world is full of skeptics like the stubborn little dwarfs. They are always looking out for themselves and are willing to play any angle that will put them ahead of anyone else. They are battling to come out on top by currying favor with those in position to help them, by stepping on those below them, and by trusting no one. When someone offers to help them, they look for his angle and are not content until they either find one or imagine one. Such behavior is contrary to the principle of love in 1 Corinthians 13. Love "does not rejoice in unrighteousness, but rejoices with the truth" (v. 6 NASB). Love "believes all things, hopes all things" (v. 7 NASB). In short, the dwarfs' kind of action has no place in the Christian life.

Another example of an individual a little too clever for his own good is Ginger the Cat. He discovers more quickly than anyone else that Shift and Rishda Tarkaan are promoting a false Aslan. He comes to this conclusion as soon as he does because he does not believe in either Aslan or Tash. And when Rishda says Aslan means no more than Tash, Ginger realizes that the Calormene, too, is an unbeliever in the supernatural. So Ginger steps right into the plot. He fabricates a story about Aslan swallowing up the bound King Tirian, and he suggests to Rishda that some of the greedier Narnians be let into the secret so they, too, can assist in the deception of those animals still loyal to Aslan. Ginger even conspires with Rishda to make use of the ape for the present, with the implication that they will eventually get rid of him.

Both Ginger and the dwarfs receive their just reward for unbelief, during the last midnight meeting at the stable. When Shift tells the beasts that a donkey has been masquerading as Aslan, Griffle shouts with a sneer that an old donkey is all Shift has ever had in the stable. Shift's response is that there is a real Tashlan inside, and anyone can go in and see him, provided they go one at a time. Griffle's cunning tells him that this is a trap, and he refuses to go to his death.

But, as prearranged, Ginger volunteers to see Tashlan. Nothing can match his smugness as he primly walks toward the stable. He knows there is a Calormene inside who will not hurt him. What he doesn't know is that Tash, whom he has really served with his lies and deception and unbelief, is also inside. Ginger does just escape becoming a meal for Tash, but he has the sense scared right out of him. The worst fate of a soulish animal, losing the ability to talk, comes upon him. It is appropriate that a creature that has lived by a wicked shrewdness should be rewarded by losing his rationality.

The dwarfs, too, are victims of their own cunning and selfishness. They try to play one side against the other so that both will be destroyed. When the Calormenes fail in their first attack, the dwarfs jeer at them, but they will not join Tirian's little army. Instead, they shoot the talking horses when it appears the balance of power may shift to Tirian's side. This turns out to be a fatal error, since Calormene reinforcements provide enough strength to hold off Tirian and take care of the dwarfs as well. Eventually, eleven of the dwarfs are thrown through the stable door.

Cunning always outsmarts itself in the end. The dwarfs make a slight miscalculation and make one side stronger than the other: the side that wants to destroy them. One of the friends of Narnia has made a slight miscalculation, too. Susan is not a shrewd person, but she, like the dwarfs and Ginger, has a warped sense of values. She turns from Aslan not so much because she doesn't believe in him as because he seems to have no relation to her social goals. She is beautiful, and beautiful girls are meant to be adored by desirable men. She fixes her attention on that and ignores everything else. Narnia becomes a game she played as a little girl.

There is a fine line to be walked between gullibility and a cunning that sees the immediate and ignores the eternal. Most of the talking animals are too gullible and accept an imitation of their beloved Aslan. The selfish ones, on the other hand, are too cunning. Ginger and the dwarfs see through the monkey's masquerade, but they ignore the real Aslan and the real Tash, to their detriment.

Tash's Revenge

The devil appears in *The Last Battle* as a vulture-headed monster named Tash. He is an idol come to life. His coming to Narnia dismays everyone who sees him. He frightens Puzzle, causes Jill to cower, and casts a deadly, foul-smelling pall over everyone in the vicinity. He does not come to Narnia unbidden. He has been called forth by the god game that Shift and Rishda Tarkaan and Ginger have been playing. None of them believes in either Aslan or Tash, but Tash makes believers of them all.

No one is more surprised than Rishda at the noise and shaking and blinding light that come when Shift is thrown into the stable. As Farsight observes, he has called on gods he did not believe in, and they have come. Tash quickly convinces him, and he proclaims his intention to offer the Narnians as a sacrifice to Tash. But Tash is not satisfied, and he takes Rishda for his own. When their captain is caught inside the stable, the other Calormenes slam the door shut and scream praises to Tash. They do not want to meet their terrible god, but they do recognize and bow down before power. All of his lawful prey is freely given to Tash, though he just misses Ginger. But when Tash turns his horrible eye on Tirian, he is dismissed by Aslan. Those who serve Tash best are destined to be devoured by him; those who are not his servants are beyond his power. It is apparent, in this instance, what the result of making a pact with the devil would be.

Blindness in Paradise

Lewis was fond of making the point that all who are in hell choose it. *The Great Divorce* describes a bus journey of condemned people who go from hell to heaven. After visiting heaven, all except one decide to go back to hell, where they are miserable and isolated, but somewhat less strained than they are in heaven. In *The Last Battle*, Lewis does something very similar with a crew of shrewd and selfish dwarfs. Really, as Eustace points out, they don't belong there at all. But Lewis has put them in Aslan's country to make a point, and they succeed in making themselves feel as wretched as they would be in hell.

Even in paradise, the dwarfs insist on being shrewd. They will not open their eyes to see the bright sky and beautiful landscape. Their mother wit tells them they are in a dark, smelly stable, so that is what they believe. Like Uncle Andrew in *The Magician's Nephew*, who hears nothing but roaring in Aslan's song of creation, the dwarfs in paradise see nothing but a stable. Whatever happens, they decide they will not be taken in again.

It is not that they are ignored, either. Lucy tells Diggle she can see his pipe, but he is not impressed, since she could smell it without seeing it. When she puts fresh flowers under his nose, he thinks he is smelling manure with a thistle in it. When Tirian talks about Aslan, Diggle is still certain that Aslan has let them down. Diggle won't open his eyes to see what Aslan has done for his servants. Even when Tirian tries to force the dwarf to notice his surroundings, Diggle only believes he has bumped against the wall of the stable. The final proof comes when Aslan sets a feast in front of the dwarfs. They first pretend to be eating filthy stable food, and then ruin their dinner by fighting over it.

What Lewis is saying is that it is just for unbelievers to be sent to hell. If they went to heaven, they would bring hell with them, in their minds. They would abide in the same darkness, have the same faults, and create the same vitriolic, warlike conditions that exist on earth. Aslan summarizes the situation well: "They will not let us help them. They have chosen cunning instead of belief. Their prison is only in their own minds, yet they are in that prison; and so afraid of being taken in that they cannot be taken out."

The Sincere Seeker

The figure of Emeth, the noble Calormene, is a difficult one to deal with. He doesn't seem to fit in with what we know about biblical truth. Jesus is the only way to life: "There is no other name under heaven that has been given among men by which we must be saved" (Acts 4:12 NASB). And yet Emeth serves Tash, or the devil, all his life and still ends up in paradise. Lewis really believed that there is only one door and that door is Jesus, but he also believed that it is possible (unlikely, but possible) to find that door even in the midst of a pagan culture.

The saga of Emeth begins with a request to enter the stable door and meet the terrible Tash face-to-face. His captain calls him a fool, but Emeth persists and is finally allowed to enter. He tells Rishda that he has always served Tash and has a strong desire to see him. He perceives that Rishda does not believe in Tash, since he flaunts him openly and is angry with Emeth for his infidelity, but Emeth knows that one unbeliever cannot cancel out a reality. When he receives his wish and goes through the door, he must fight for his life, but not with Tash. Having killed the man guarding the door, he wanders off in a daze, through Aslan's country, looking for Tash. When he finally meets Aslan, he knows immediately that he has been wrong all his life and that Aslan is worthy of all honor.

Emeth expects to die on the spot, but just as he used to consider one glimpse of Tash worth the probability of death, so, now, seeing Aslan is worth his expected punishment for unbelief. But, to his surprise, Aslan informs Emeth that he is not really an infidel. Because Tash is utterly vile and Aslan is completely good, no good service can be done to Tash, and no bad service can be done to Aslan. Thus, Aslan rewards those who keep their oaths sworn by Tash, because that is a good deed; and Tash accepts the deeds of those who are cruel in Aslan's name.

Lewis is not denying salvation by grace through faith. Nor is he preaching a doctrine of salvation by works. He does indicate that there is a strong implication that Emeth would have accepted Aslan, if the lion had been fairly presented to him as the way to life. Emeth recognizes this at once when he meets Aslan face-to-face and would probably have done so if he had had a chance to spend much time in Narnia. There have been native villages where the claims of Christ have been presented for the first time, but the natives already seemed to know about Him. In one case, the response to a missionary's message was, "Oh, yes, we know who He is, but we didn't know His name." Apparently, it is possible, though not likely, to discover who Christ is without coming in direct contact with Christians. Paul says there are signs in the universe that hint of divine reality. If these signs are followed faithfully, one can arrive at the truth.

The second point he is making is that specific words really have no meaning, until they are given meaning by associated ideas, circumstances, and events. The words *Jesus* and *Christ*, for example, differ slightly in sound in various languages, but those words in any language take on meaning only as they are associated with concepts such as sin, sacrifice, incarnation, salvation, death, resurrection, ascension, and return. If, in some far-removed land, all of the events and characteristics associated with Christ by the Bible were translated by the word *Satan*, then *Satan* would mean "Christ" in that language. That, in effect, is what has happened to Emeth. He thinks he is committed to Tash, but he has imputed Aslan's characteristics to Tash. He has learned to do good acts through personal contact with the spirit of the lion. Thus, when he sees Aslan, he recognizes at once the object of his devotion, though he expects retribution for calling him the wrong name. But God does, indeed, look on the heart.

A person can't get to heaven by acting like the devil. Using God-words to justify corrupt behavior won't help, either. First John makes quite clear that the Christian is characterized by love. The person who is committed to Christ shows more and more love in his day-to-day interaction with friends and neighbors. The one who says he is of God but has no love is not one of His. Rishda Tarkaan, Shift, and Ginger fall into this category. It is not that men are earning salvation, since no one is capable of that. It is just that the God of love is inside believers, and He will show through unless Christians totally bottle Him up.

Emeth should not give hope to the outwardly virtuous person who rejects Christianity. Emeth has not accepted Aslan, because he has never heard. He is not an irreligious person; he doesn't just do what he feels is right. He is active in his devotion to as much of God as he can perceive. Had Aslan's claims been presented to Emeth and had Emeth turned the lion away, he would have been lost. But because Emeth walked in the light he had and would have accepted Aslan, he receives eternal life.

Making an End

Anyone who has had a beautiful experience or has been in a beautiful place wants it to last forever. Jill is no exception. When Jewel tells her about all the peaceful years in Narnia that have unfolded between visits from children of this world, Jill wishes that, unlike earth, Narnia could last forever. But Jewel tells her that all worlds come to an end, except Aslan's own country. When Farsight tells them of the rout at Cair Paravel, they realize the truth of Roonwit's dying reminder that "all worlds draw to an end and that noble death is a treasure which no one is too poor to buy." Some of them buy that treasure through battle, and the rest pass out of Narnia into paradise through the stable door. But all are present as Aslan makes an end to Narnia. In a way, the destruction of Narnia parallels its creation; it is prefaced by the horn of Father Time, rather than by the song of Aslan, which called Narnia into being. The first effect of Aslan's song was to call the stars into being, and the initial result of Father Time's horn is to cause the stars to fall; next, Father Time's horn calls to life the huge monsters that have been sleeping with him under the northern waste. Jill and Eustace had seen them sleeping there on their journey in search of Prince Rilian.

The monsters scare all the soulish creatures toward Aslan for the Narnian version of the final judgment. Once again Lewis combines the seemingly contradictory concepts of fear and love. All the soulish creatures are impelled toward him by fear. They have no choice about that, just as they have no choice about looking him in the face as they approach. Where they do have a choice is in hating or loving him. Those who love him pass into paradise, and those who hate him pass into his dark shadow and disappear. The talking animals who hate him show hatred for only a moment and then cease to be able to talk.

Lewis gives an instructive parallel to Jesus' prophesied separation of the sheep and the goats: "And all the nations will be gathered before Him; and He will separate them from one another, as the shepherd separates the sheep from the goats; and He will put the sheep on His right, and the goats on the left" (Matt. 25:32–33 NASB). Then Christ accepts the sheep and tells them they have ministered to Him through ministering to those who are needy. Likewise, He rejects the goats and informs them they have neglected Him by neglecting the needy. This may seem to differ from Lewis's criterion of love for Aslan, but there really is no substantial difference. Those who have been filled with Christ's love will minister in love to those who need it, and those who have been filled with Satan's hatred will minister that to those in need.

Some surprising characters are allowed to enter the door. One of the dwarfs who shot the horses and who was part of the group that scoffed against Aslan is there. This emphasizes once again God's capacity for mercy. Unlike Poggin, this dwarf did not break from his fellows while in Narnia, but presumably he stayed with the others through weakness and not through contempt or hatred for Aslan.

The Narnian monsters next begin to tear up and snap the trees, and the grass withers and dies in a continued reversal of Aslan's creation song. Eventually Narnia is as bare and lifeless as the day Digory and Polly arrived. After a flood sweeps over the landscape, it only remains to put out the sun and moon. The sun gathers the moon into itself, and Father Time reaches out and squeezes the old sun like an orange until it, too, goes out. Then Peter, the High King, pulls the stable door shut, and

Narnia is no more. Jill and Eustace and even Tirian cannot help mourning for the beloved country. Tirian says that it would be discourtesy to Narnia not to mourn its passing.

The Holidays Begin

C. S. Lewis gives an absolutely glorious picture of heaven in *The Last Battle*. After reading his description, it may be difficult to think of heaven except in terms of Aslan's country.

Concerning the point of transition from earthly life, through death, to heavenly life, Edmund confirms the idea that it is much easier for a believer to die a sudden death than it is for one to live after a beloved person has passed on. Edmund is briefly aware of an impact, then he feels all of his pain go away, and finally he is free and light in his new, perfect body. On his part there has been no suffering.

When Aslan's people come to the tree Digory took fruit from in *The Magician's Nephew*, they discover that its fruits are typical of that whole country. The fruit is so delectable that they wonder whether it can be right to take one. But, as Peter informs his companions, they have come to the place where, if they want anything, it is right to have it. The thought of that—the country where everything is allowed—is breathtaking. Just to be able to do what one wants and not to have to think whether or not that desire is right must be an exhilarating feeling. Of course, the reason Peter is right is because people's minds, as well as their bodies, will be made flawless in heaven.

The only real command that seems to apply in Aslan's country is to go "further up and further in." When the talking animals and humans obey this command, they discover two things: The real Narnia, the one that has always existed and after which the familiar Narnia was patterned, is still there to be enjoyed; and here, too, the inside is bigger than the outside. Lewis has used these two concepts before.

Although Narnia has been destroyed, that which was perfect about it is still in existence, and everything about the new Narnia is larger than it was before. Heaven is the archetype, and earth is only a shallow reflection of it. The world that will pass away should not be grieved after, because heaven will be much more than any other world.

Just as the inside of the wardrobe was much bigger than the outside, since it contained all of Narnia, so the inside of the stable is bigger than the outside, since it contains a heavenly Narnia on a grander and more perfect scale than the one that soon ends. And the inside of the garden on the green hill turns out to be bigger than that newly discovered Narnia.

Heaven is not going to be a boring place. The more one learns about it, the more he shall find to learn. Much of the redeemed person's interest will be focused on the simple and delightful act of discovering what the Lord has provided for him there. No one will just be relegated to second harp in the third heavenly choir. There will be an eternity of things to see and do, such as running like the wind without tiring (a literal fulfillment of Isa. 40:31). And all the things a believer discovers will testify to the love and power and creativity of God.

Best of all is the fact that going "further up and further in" leads to the initiator of all of these marvelous things. Aslan greets his visitors and tells them that they can say good-bye to shadow-lands once and for all. Then he no longer appears to them as a lion, and it is understood, though Lewis doesn't say it, that Aslan has all along been a fantasy form of Christ. Lucy says once before that the inside of a stable was bigger than the whole world; she is referring to Jesus' birthplace. There are infinite wonders to be discovered in Him. The real adventure behind Narnia is knowing, loving, and serving Him. Nothing else matters, or it matters only in relation to that great commitment. We, too, can experience the deep joy that throbs through Lucy's voice, but only if we go further up and further in to a deeper commitment to and knowledge of God. In that knowledge there are pleasures forevermore, and that commitment is the meaning of life itself.

Paul Karkainen discovered C. S. Lewis in college and has been reading this prolific author ever since. Paul has degrees in English literature from Whitworth College (BA) and the University of Oregon (MA) and a master's degree in public administration from the University of Washington.

Paul appreciates all three sides of the Lewis triangle: the imaginative creator of fantasy worlds, the incisive literary critic, and the profound philosopher and theologian. However, it is the pervasive presence of Aslan and his realm of talking animals that has reverberated through Paul's mind for the past forty years. Almost daily, some situation in Paul's life reminds him of a Narnian event or truism. He and his wife, Carolyn, have three adult children—Amie, Ryan, and Karl—who are also fans of Narnia.

Paul and his family revel in hiking the Cascades, biking, reading, and taking daily walks with their tawny Labrador retriever, Angel. They reside in Washington.